# Handsome Is

# Handsome Is

## Adventures with Saul Bellow

*a memoir by*

## Harriet Wasserman

FROMM INTERNATIONAL PUBLISHING CORPORATION
NEW YORK

First Edition 1997
Library of Congress Cataloging-in-Publication Data

Wasserman, Harriet.
    Handsome is : adventures with Saul Bellow / Harriet Wasserman.
        p.   cm.
    ISBN 0-88064-177-0
    1. Bellow, Saul—Friends and associates.   2. Novelists, American—
20th century—Biography.   3. Wasserman, Harriet—Friends and
associates.   4. Literary agents—United States—Biography.
I. Title.
PS3503.E4488Z92  1997
813'.52—dc21
    [B]                                                   96-37386
                                                            CIP


10  9  8  7  6  5  4  3  2  1

Manufactured in the United States

# Acknowledgment

Candida Donadio

C.M.S.

T.H.G.

# Contents

third (Lily), and fourth (Eden) grandchildren; receive the Nobel Prize; go to the movies; grieve over the death in the Israeli army of the son of his dear friend John Auerbach, and fly off to be at John's side; grieve over the death of his nephew, Jane's son Bobby, from AIDS and over old friends "dropping all around as on a battlefield"; read aloud from the Bible, Balzac, Whitman, and Austen; recite his translation into Yiddish of T.S. Eliot's "Prufrock"; suffer from Seasonal Affective Disorder whenever there's a cloudy day; shop for garlic presses, French *tarte* pans, red socks, secondhand books; give guided tours in his car of Chicago streets, pointing out places, special in his life, where once stood his high school, etc., now broken-down neighborhoods and slums "worse than any in New York City"; swat flies and keep score; shake a leafy branch over his shoulder, as he'd seen African elephants do, while walking through the woods on hot insect-swarmy days, a most effective natural repellent; test-squeeze melons for ripeness at the local fruit stand; find an optometrist on Lexington Avenue who still sold monocles, to fulfill a longtime wish, after winning the Nobel Prize, to be able to release, no hands, the glass from his eye socket straight into his breast pocket, a trick he'd seen an old professor do; visit accountants, lawyers, colleagues, writers, students, relatives, friends, and publishers, the latter almost always unannounced; have temper tantrums of proportions mild and fleeting as summer squalls to terrifying and apoplectic.

And all the while endless conversation, on every level, about Robin Williams, the Chicago Bulls, the Celtics, tat-

toos and lip rings, free radicals and antioxidants, the after-
life, ethics, outer space, his grade school teachers' names,
the items on his sister's dressing table when she was a
teenager, Elmore Leonard, Stendhal, Marilyn Monroe,
Frank Sinatra, Nathan Detroit, Ann Landers, Jesse Jackson,
Jackie Onassis, Cardinal Lustiger, Dr. Ruth, Jung, James
Bond, Gucci, Bergdorf Goodman, Dr. Scholl's foot pads,
Simone de Beauvior, Wimbledon, Goldenberg's Peanut
Chews, Melville, Proust, Joyce, Samuel Beckett, Yasir Arafat,
Yitzhak Rabin, Mitterrand, Wordsworth, Robert Lowell,
Allen Ginsberg, Rudolf Steiner, and on and on and on.

Saul Bellow's relationships, in his books and in his life—
one and the same really, with women especially—are subject to much speculation and interest by the public. His
critics have characterized him as a "womanizer," "misogy-
nist," "male chauvinist," etc. However, for three decades he
entrusted his work to a young woman (now, as Saul would
describe it, "in the full bloom of her maturity"), whose
career, indeed, he helped to start.

Somewhere midway in our association, Saul described
me to myself as "a museum piece trapped inside a middle-
class liberal Jewish girl, living in a ghost town of virtue." I
certainly toughened from the timid, naive soul, to express-
ing myself, standing up for myself, and even, on occasion,
giving back as good as I got.

"Okay, Harriet, you made your point. Do you want to
start Round Two now?"

# *I.*

## Handsome Is

*O*n July 1, 1995, marking the occasion of the thirtieth anniversary of my days as a literary agent, it came to me in a flash that all that time I've been a real-life character in a living Saul Bellow novel.

Four years after I joined Russell & Volkening Literary Representatives as an assistant, Saul Bellow visited the office of his longtime agent, Henry Volkening, and jump-started my career by pointing out to Henry and his partner, Diarmuid (pronounced "Dermott") Russell, "Pay attention to her—she's got something there."

From my first week at the agency, whenever Saul called and I'd answer the phone, he'd make comments such as: "Oh, this is Russell & Volkening? It sounds like Mrs. Ross's sewing circle." The two or three times a year he'd come in, he'd announce: "Just a minute—I have to go and flirt with Harriet first."

One January day in 1969, he came to have lunch with his agent at the Century Club—or, as Henry phrased it, to have "drunch at the Drenchery Club." Saul knew he'd not get anything to eat before Henry had a few Old Grand-Dads, so he'd always grab a sandwich at the Horn & Hardart's across the street beforehand. At our agency, all of the offices were doorless and lined up in a row: Henry's, Diarmuid's, mine. That day, Saul stopped in front of mine. I was on the phone. He came in and looked me over—up and down. I was skinny then, and I was wearing a great dress. He came behind me, to my free ear: "You know, you're really very pretty. Do you think you could take care of me? Would you marry me?" I took it lightly, laughed it off.

Back from lunch, Henry stood within earshot of Diarmuid's office and said in a loud voice, "Saul says Harriet has a pure heart. He says we should pay attention to her—she's got something there."

Diarmuid popped up from his crossword puzzle.

He always finished his letters and cleared his desk by 11:30 A.M., and then he'd do his puzzle from the *Guardian*, his feet resting in his bottom desk drawer. He was very tall and handsome, an outdoorsman type. His father was the poet AE, and "Uncle Bill" was William Butler Yeats. Those two had been the editors of the *Irish Statesman* together. Diarmuid was a close friend of David Rockefeller, but he kept an account on his calendar of every cent I owed him: "HW 1¢ lunch." He wore the same raincoat for twenty years. It was pretty grubby. One day, he walked in and it was very wrinkled but clean. He was so happy: He'd found out, after twenty years, that it could be washed rather than dry-cleaned, which "saves money."

Henry was the exact opposite. He was a little, indoors guy. Henry wrote long, long, gushy letters to clients and editors, Diarmuid wrote one-line notes: "Dear Craig. Enclosed a Welty. Yours, Diarmuid."

The partners hadn't spoken for years, and this was their means of communication—proclamations in the hallway. Saul used to say, "Henry and Diarmuid don't run a literary agency, they run an eighteenth-century British vinegar distillery."

But when Henry called out, "Saul says Harriet has a pure heart. He says we should pay attention to her . . ." Diarmuid jumped up and said out loud, "Saul's in love with Harriet."

And from then on they paid attention to me.

In the course of that afternoon, Saul came back to my office three times, sat down in the chair facing me: "Come with me to London tonight" . . . "Have you got a passport?" . . . "Let's go to your apartment and get your passport." Laughing and pointing at my instrument case, I said, "I've got a rehearsal tonight with the Collegium of New York Pro Musica." When he returned from London, he said he felt bad, felt I had been laughing at him.

I had no self-confidence. I graduated Hunter College magna cum laude and Phi Beta Kappa with a major in political science, but it didn't seem like something I had achieved. Instead, it seemed like some kind of fluke. When Saul told Henry, "she's got something there," it became a call for me to rise to his expectations. That was the basis of a lot of my feelings for him. He gave me a real classical education in art and spirit. He was my mentor. Our close business association and friendship (at a reception in Houston in 1988, Saul referred to me as "coach, manager, and trainer") began most improbably, in the last years of Henry and Diarmuid's partnership, indeed, their lives.

By the beginning of the seventies, to all intents and purposes, I was already acting as Saul's agent. Saul came to New York from Chicago one freezing February day in

1972 to give me 135 pages of an early draft of *Humboldt's Gift*. It was then that I realized he was counting on me as first reader. Late one afternoon, an assistant at Russell & Volkening said: "God's on the phone at La Guardia Airport. He wants you to meet him in front of the Westbury at six-thirty to pick up the manuscript pages." The traffic was bad, and the taxicab fairy was definitely not on my side. When I got there, a little late, Saul was standing, freezing, out in front of the hotel, without a hat, which was unusual. His nose was red and watery. I took the manuscript of *Humboldt's Gift* and continued on home in the cab.

Even though I had read all of his published work, being handed this manuscript was something special. It was late at night, and I was exhausted, very excited, and somewhat nervous about reading it, as if I were back in school, being tested. But once I started, I couldn't put it down. I loved it. It opened something like: "I, Charlie Citrine, the lanky son of an immigrant who came with nothing but a rolled-up mattress to Ellis Island . . ." It was very breezy, very high-spirited. When Saul revises, he usually revises from the beginning, so this early opening was nothing like the published version. But it was so enjoyable, I read it through that night. I always like to read a manuscript in one sitting, and twice before responding. I got up early Saturday morning to do the second read, so I'd be fluent in it when I spoke with Saul that evening.

He was coming for dinner. Not only was I reading his manuscript pages for the first time, but he was coming to my apartment for the first time. I was busy shopping and getting my hair done and figuring out what to wear. I still didn't get it: the fact that my reading was important to him and that was why he'd come to New York. I was more concerned with vacuuming.

At about four that afternoon, he called up and said, "I'm at the Strand." (The largest used bookstore in the world: "8 miles of books," often frequented by writers.) The manager, Burt Britton, was putting together a book of self-portraits by writers, and he'd got Saul to do one. "Can I come up now?"

"My apartment is a mess."

"I'm freezing. I don't care what your rug looks like."

I asked him to come at five. I had expected him at six-thirty and was completely discombobulated. I kept cutting myself trying to shave my legs.

By the time he rang my doorbell, I realized the food wasn't out of the freezer. I shoved the vacuum into the closet. I was wearing a body suit and threw the caftan I'd just bought at Bloomingdale's over it. He walked in, and the first thing he said was, "Boy, you're cold—not a word about my book." Which didn't do much good for my nerves, either. "You didn't call last night," he said, "or this morning. And you didn't say anything when I called you from the Strand."

Saul's a literary idol and an electric, formidable presence. I was a babe in the woods, socially backward, even for the ideal mid-twentieth-century "good girl." He's always dressed like nobody else. He has great taste in clothes, slightly far-out: always a great tie you'd never see before or after, great colors in shirts, suits with knock-out linings, flashy but in good taste too. His style makes him look taller than he is. He's about five feet seven, and I realized after a while that he was self-conscious about his height. There's not a protagonist in any of his work who is under six feet tall. Writer Bob Gutwillig, back in those days, meeting Saul in a bar for an interview, later described him as "alarmingly handsome."

Henry wasn't the only one who'd break out in sweats when Saul came to town. He intimidated everyone. Years later, the photographer Tom Victor, who took many wonderful photos of Saul, said to me, before a photo session at Tom's studio on Twentieth Street and Fifth Avenue: "Saul looks at you like the strictest teacher you ever had in school. The one you were most afraid of." He has a way of giving a look—sharp and penetrating—that can scare you to death, a no-place-to-hide feeling. For Saul, having his picture taken is like going to the dentist. "I'm not going to stay here long. I'm not going to take my coat off." He was like a little boy. I did go to the dentist with him once— my dentist—just before a taping of *The Dick Cavett Show* in December 1981. He had trouble with an abscessed tooth. He went into the waiting room and refused to take his down coat off. He wanted to leave. Having his photo taken for book jackets was the same thing.

Tom Victor would say, "Okay, okay, Saul. I'll be quick. I'll work like a dog."

Saul: "If you work like a dog, I'll sit like a dog."

Tom was always concerned about Saul's wattles and jowls. No matter how high he told Saul to hold up his chin, those jowls were still hanging there. Finally, at a session where he had to work like a dog, Tom put the lights on, went over to Saul, grabbed the loose skin, shoved it down under his shirt collar and tightened Saul's tie. He did it so fast, Saul hardly realized what was going on, before it was all over and Tom started shooting.

When Saul told me I had been cold by not responding immediately to *Humboldt's Gift*, I understood that I had become his first reader and that what he needed from me was my honest response. He was counting on me for that. Thereafter, for the next twenty-five years, as he gave me pages to read, I'd call at once with a response, no matter what the time of day or night. And I'd tell him I'd get back to him after I read the draft twice more.

On that freezing February night, I sat down on my couch, and Saul sat in a rocking chair facing me, and I gave him my response to his pages. I made a criticism about his character Charlie Citrine. Charlie says, "Every time I go into the elevator and the door opens, I expect to see a beautiful woman." "Why does it always have to be a beautiful woman?" I said. "Why can't it be a woman?"

"What's the matter with that?" Saul said gruffly. But he had asked for my opinion. By then I had given the pages a good reading, and he knew that I understood them.

Then he said he was hungry. I went into the kitchen. I hadn't set the table. I realized that I'd left the *saucisson en croûte* in the freezer. I was in a sweaty panic. The *boeuf bourguignon* and the rice and vegetables were out, and I got them into pots. From the living room, Saul asked about my recorders—he plays the recorder too. There I was, in the kitchen, frazzled but at least alone, convincing myself, like the Little Engine That Could, that I'd be able to get something together. What did he do? He picked up my soprano recorder and stood at the kitchen doorway, watching me and playing tunes the whole time.

We sat down to dinner in my glass conservatory, nineteen stories up, with its imposing close-up view of the Empire State Building. He liked that a lot. While we were eating, he said, "What's the matter? You seem distracted."

"I'm okay."

"I know what it is. You're distracted because you're nervous. You don't know if we're going to make love or not."

My response to that was reflex action. I dropped my fork on my plate, and my knife landed on the floor. They both made a clink. He started laughing. It was comical. Obviously, I was nervous . . . and flustered.

Then we had coffee and dessert and came into the living room. He took his shoes off, lay down on my couch, and put his hands behind his head. He started wiggling his toes. He said, "You see these feet of clay? Do you want to touch these feet of clay?" He had his socks on.

He asked me to come to the couch and sit by him. When I did, he reached over and gave me a kiss. I had on Max Factor Grape lipstick. "Are you chewing bubble gum? You taste just like bubble gum!"

Meanwhile, I'm thinking: Oh my God, should we or shouldn't we? Is this good for business?

The point of no return came when Saul got up and walked right over to my bed. My studio apartment was quite big, but there was no door to go through—he could just walk right over to the bed. Then I knew it wasn't going to be good for business either way. I was in a panic.

I had worn a black Lastex body suit under my caftan because I didn't think it would be good for business. Oh my God, I'm going to lose my client, my career is going to go down the drain. It was one thing to take off the caftan, but I didn't dare take off the body suit.

"You're not coming to bed in that diving suit!" he told me.

"It has a zipper."

"What?" Then he said, "I'm not judging you."

Not much.

By this time, I'm muttering it out loud. "Is this good for business? Is this good for business?" Suddenly in my head it's the night of the Miss America pageant, and I had somehow gotten onstage.

When we were in bed, the red light on the Empire State Building tower was blinking at us. I kept asking him for permission, as if he were a museum objet d'art.

"Can I touch this?"

"Yes."

"Can I touch this?"

"Yes."

Then I found myself saying, "Ooh! You had an appendectomy!"

He rolled his eyes upward.

When he left that night, I walked him to the elevator, thinking, "I've just lost a client, I've just lost a job. And as the elevator door closed, he said, "You were really cold to me." That's how he left.

The next day, I went to see him to return the glove he had forgotten. I didn't know what to expect. He said he hadn't had a date like that since under the Coney Island boardwalk when he was in high school. "I almost laughed," he said, "but I didn't want to hurt your feelings." I said I almost laughed too. But for me it had been a comic nightmare. He was this great famous man. And I— who had been so torn between should I or shouldn't I— knew, no matter what he said, or because of what he did say, that he was judging me.

That night was never mentioned again. As if it never happened. At all. It wasn't in our eyes. It wasn't in our tone of voice. There was no flirting anymore. It was strictly business—and a growing friendship.

In fact, as both Henry's and Diarmuid's health failed, they knew they would have to sell the agency and wanted me to buy them out. They had tried to sell the business for $150,000, and that hadn't worked. Henry called me in and put on a piece of paper in pencil the price I'd have to pay for his half. I read it in my office: "$25,000 in cash, Punkt." "Oh, no, Henry, I couldn't do that. It's worth much more. Oh, no." Then Diarmuid called me in. For his half he wanted $75,000. Looking back on it, I realize he hadn't budged from his original asking price. Diarmuid wanted to help me buy the business and offered to take me to see Mr. Lord at the Morgan Guaranty Bank at Forty-fourth Street and Fifth Avenue, where Russell & Volkening had had an account since opening day in May 1940. Diarmuid knew they were both really ready to pass down the mantle and felt that with the way things were going, I'd probably be able to pay back a loan on what the agency would bring in during the next year or two. I think he understood the opportunity I was passing up. He was furious at my reluctance. But the truth was, I was a woman-child of the fifties and scared. But at the same time I thought: Can you make it 51 percent? I didn't want to buy half. Suppose I, too, got myself in a position in which I would be stuck with an unwanted equal partner?

For a while I had backers. But when they came to the office and saw how frail Diarmuid and Henry looked, they advised me to wait six months, when they thought it could be got for less, and backed out.

Diarmuid and Henry wanted the business to go on, and they had the faith in me that I didn't have. I simply wasn't ready.

Theirs had been an improbable partnership from the beginning. Henry told me his version one afternoon in 1971, after George Panetta's funeral in Brooklyn. George was a client. When he decided to write children's books, Henry handed him over to me, and I took him to lunch as his agent. Afterward, when I picked up the check, George was taken aback. "A dame!" he said in pronounced Brooklynese. "A dame? Ooh, I never had a dame pay for anything. You're actually going to pick up the check? A dame taking me to lunch—how do you like that?"

Henry and I took the subway back from Brooklyn to Lüchow's, the historic German restaurant on Fourteenth Street, and Henry talked about himself.

He was from Yorkville, the German section of Manhattan.

His grandfather had served in the German Army in the First World War. As an American kid, Henry felt torn, but it was his grandfather, and he loved him. His classmates taunted him, and he himself was haunted for the rest of his life about a Jewish classmate (Princeton '23) whom all the Princetonians razzed. He told me that story often.

I think my presence always reminded Henry, and he wished he could redo and make amends.

Saul Bellow was Henry's client, and Bernard Malamud was Diarmuid's. They were representative Male Jewish American Novelists at the time when MJANs were the high point of our culture. It was a duel. Diarmuid used Bernard as his sword and Henry used Saul.

Henry had read a Saul Bellow story in Harper's Bazaar and wrote offering his services, which were accepted. The first two novels, Dangling Man and The Victim, had been published by Vanguard Press in 1944 and 1947, without benefit of representation. Henry recommended George Joel at The Dial Press and Harold Guinzburg at The Viking Press, Saul chose the latter in 1948, and his work was published by Viking for the next thirty years.

Henry's first client was Michael Seide, whose collection of short stories, entitled The Common Thread, Henry sold to Doubleday. Seide recommended his agent to his friend Bernard Malamud, with whom he was teaching in the English department at a high school in Manhattan. However, Malamud became a lifelong client of Diarmuid.

"How come?" I asked.

"When Bernard called, I answered the phone," answered Diarmuid.

In the following years, Henry tried and tried, but Seide never had another book published. After three years of trying, Diarmuid finally sold a Malamud story, then a novel, *The Natural*, and on to National Book Award, Pulitzer Prize, American Academy of Arts & Letters Gold Medal, etc., etc.

That afternoon at Lüchow's, Henry talked effusively about Mr. *Sammler's Planet*, which had been published recently. He kept saying "Artoor," pronouncing Mr. Sammler's given name as Mr. Sammler did: not Arthur, but "Artur." Henry used to get on jags like that. He told me he and Thomas Wolfe used to eat at Lüchow's and then go to the burlesque on Fourteenth Street. Henry was just out of Fordham Law and working in real estate, which he didn't like at all. He taught night school at NYU, where Wolfe was on the faculty too. They had become buddies, and it was Tom who suggested that Henry go and talk to his editor, the renowned Maxwell Perkins, about getting into publishing. Perkins told him he didn't have an editorial opening, then suggested he consider becoming an agent.

A month or so later, Diarmuid Russell came in to see Maxwell Perkins. Diarmuid, then an editor at Putnam, asked Perkins for advice on becoming an agent. Many years afterward, Diarmuid told me Perkins had said, "There are too many damn agents already, but just the other week there was a gent who came to see me. Maybe you ought to get together with him."

Shortly thereafter, in May 1940, Henry and Diarmuid began their partnership. They each put up five thousand dollars.

Their only criterion for taking on representation of a writer was their belief in the work's high literary quality. They never compromised for commercial reasons. Once they made their commitment, their faith in the author and the work was unshakable, and eventually was rewarded, sometimes after years of rejection after rejection.

From reading R&V's book and manuscript library, I developed a taste for the true, the real thing and became a snob fortunate enough to represent only writers and work I truly love.

Scott Berg, who wrote the best-selling biography of Maxwell Perkins published in the mid-seventies, quoted Perkins as saying, "There are too damn many women agents already." When he came to the office (by now he was an R&V client), I told Scott he had that wrong. That Diarmuid himself told me the story, and Perkins had said, "'There are too many agents already,' not women agents. I remember it distinctly." But Scott insisted, he said he knew for sure. "No," I said, "I know for sure." I went back to my office and sat down, and it occurred to me that, of course, Diarmuid wouldn't have told me Perkins said there were too damn many women agents already! I ran out to catch Scott at the elevator. "Oh, God, I just got it!"

Henry took his vacation every July, Diarmuid every August. One July day, a young woman writer, very enthusiastic and bubbly, walked straight into Diarmuid's office—as I said, none of our offices had doors. "Are you Henry Volkening? I've just come from Chicago especially to meet you, and I'm so excited and thrilled."

"No, I'm not Henry Volkening." Diarmuid looked up from his crossword puzzle. "You'll have to come back in August if you want to see him!" The young woman was somewhat taken aback by the cold reception. She was used to Henry's effusive letters. She asked, "Well, do you happen to have a picture of Henry Volkening?"

"What would I want with a picture of my partner? If I want to see him, I can just go next door and look!"

Henry kept all the records of earnings. Each author had a five-by-seven paper slip from a white scratch pad, and Henry would note the earnings through the year and then tally them up in pencil. Russell & Volkening didn't have an adding machine. As I understood it from Henry at Lüchow's, one year in the fifties he got back from his vacation and found that Diarmuid had kept the records and left him a note that said, "My clients did better than your clients this year." That was it. Henry never spoke directly to him again to his dying day. Diarmuid never had a clue why.

Saul wasn't much more fond of Diarmuid than Henry was. One day in the late sixties, Saul came into the office and Diarmuid said, "Oh, that's a gay tie you're wearing." Saul asked, "In the old sense or the new sense?"

Diarmuid: "There's a new sense?"

Saul had two grudges against Diarmuid. His daughter, Pam, had rented Saul's house in Tivoli, New York, one summer and according to Saul trampled his garden. And once, when Henry was on vacation, Diarmuid sent Saul some Italian tax forms to be signed and didn't enclose a stamped, self-addressed envelope. Saul was enraged. I made a mental note and have always sent my clients SASEs.

Henry's moods were erratic. Sometimes he would come back from the Drenchery Club holding on to the walls till he got to my office, where he'd be jolly and ebullient. At other times, he'd return morose. He would perform mock trials at moot court. He had a law degree, and he would pull out all the stops, often sweeping his glasses off and gesturing with them in his hand, then dramatically returning them to his face. He'd call witnesses, he'd cross-examine them. He'd win every case brilliantly and return to his own office in triumph.

Once, Henry came back from lunch very upset and told me an editor had double-crossed him and that Henry refused to send him any more manuscripts. Several months later, the editor asked him for lunch, and Henry accepted.

He was in one of his up moods when he returned to the office. The editor had pleaded with him to send manuscripts. "Mea culpa," he said. It would never happen again.

"I know, I know. I know it won't ever happen again," Henry said at the end of the meal. "I know because I'm not ever going to give you the opportunity."

I picked up another clue from Henry. Thanks for the warning: "I know you'll never do it again. I'm absolutely sure of it. I'm not ever going to give you the chance."

Henry always boasted that he never told a lie and advised three reasons. One: You'll sleep better at night. Two: You won't have to remember what you said. Three: No one will believe you anyway.

In January 1970, Henry's wife, Natalie, came back from a Caribbean cruise coughing; she died of lung cancer in May. Henry was lost without Natalie, and in the fall, he too was found to have a lung tumor. When Saul came into the office at the beginning of 1972, he expressed his condolences. "What a horrible year." It had been a lousy one for him too. "Well, Henry, there's one good thing about the year 1971. It won't be the year on our tombstone." Thereafter, Saul would recite that line to me on his first phone call of every new year.

Henry smoked like a chimney, so did Diarmuid. Natalie died of secondhand smoke. I visited Henry at Lenox Hill Hospital. Not only was he very sick, but he had lost his will to live. He didn't talk, he had withdrawn from life. I returned to Diarmuid to report that Henry's cancer was inoperable, and that though no one would tell him straight out, he knew full well there was no chance of recovery.

As I left Henry in his room, I imagined that his spirit had already packed up and moved on, and he was gone from the corporeal realm. When his daughter, Joyce, came to see him at home the following week, he did not recognize her and was silent.

A week later, Diarmuid called me into his office. He was smiling oddly. He'd just gotten the results of some tests, and his doctors told him he had the exact same kind of lung cancer as Henry. When, just eight days before, I had given him a detailed account of Henry's prognosis, he was ironically amused. Had I known, I would of course have left room for optimism, if not hope. He was stoical.

The two of them held on, so they could keep an eye on each other.

Diarmuid had always said that I was "ambitious in a nice way." I never thought of myself as being ambitious. I didn't consciously plan ahead: I'm going to do this, I'm going to do that. I never planned to have a career. Though even to this day, probably, no one grows up wanting to be a literary agent, and certainly in my time few (I am one of them) knew there was any such thing in the world, it was as though I had entered a revolving door and never found my way out again. I thought it was just something temporary, until my real life started.

At that time, I called Saul and told him I was coming to Chicago on my way to a recorder workshop in Minnesota, and could we have dinner together. This was before that freezing February night *chez moi*.

I met him at his apartment in the Cloisters, the huge South Side complex near the University of Chicago. A graduate student was just on her way out. Saul was wearing a white shirt and a tie, no jacket, and his cheeks were flushed. He noticed that I was looking very intently at an engraving on the foyer wall.

It was a very *zaftig* nude woman.

"That's Rembrandt."

I must have had a bemused expression on my face.

"The *artist* is Rembrandt."

In the elevator, a woman got on, and behind her back Saul put his hands in his ears, stuck his tongue out, and wiggled his fingers. When she got out, he said, "I wouldn't touch her with a ten-foot pole." I looked down and said, "Do you have a ten-foot pole?" A Mae West sort of thing. It just came out of my mouth. I think I was trying to be sophisticated. He looked very surprised. Raised his eyebrows.

We went to a Chinese restaurant, "a joint" near the campus, under the El. Seated across from me in a booth, he said, "Are you here to truss me up and deliver me? You know Doubleday directly offered me a two-book contract for two hundred thousand dollars and promised to get me a summer house in Spain." Obviously, the prospect was alluring.

I told Saul: Of course, you have to consider that. But whoever and whatever you choose, if you decide to stay with R&V or not, be aware of the terms, especially with a two-book contract. Foremost to consider: a provision that if book number one earns out before you deliver

book number two, the contract separates into two indi-
vidual contracts. Otherwise, the earnings from book
number one will pay for the advance of book number
two. I think he got it. A gleam came into his eye. "Oh."

I told him about percentages and about escalated splits
on paperback royalties. Don't concentrate on the house in
Spain. Forget that fantasy. The important thing is to have
a good publisher, who would give you the best possible
publication. You can always buy your own house in
Spain.

I was very cool. No pressure. My intuition told me that
was the way the author would consider it. I would never
come on strong anyway. That's not me. I played it very cool.
It would seem it worked.

Then we got into his car and he drove me back to my
hotel. He stopped in front of the hotel, reached over, and
gave me a peck on the cheek. "Thank you," I said.

"Thank you?"

I think he meant it as a compliment.

# II.

## To Almería and Back

*H*enry Volkening was seventy and Diarmuid Russell seventy-one when they died, within a year after they had sold the agency in the summer of '72. The new owner's promise to me of a partnership never was fulfilled. He was new to the literary agenting trade and asked me to "show him the ropes." I had become Saul's exclusive agent as well as his first reader. Saul knew I was going to Spain to visit a client in Barcelona in the summer of 1974, and he invited me to the house he had rented outside Almería, where he was working toward the completion of *Humboldt's Gift*. He had stayed several seasons previously at the summer home of his old friend and British publisher, Barley Alison, about whom he frequently spoke. I hadn't met her, but I knew her house overlooked the Mediterranean, and the one he rented was close by. "Oh, why don't you come down and visit," he said, and sent me possible dates. They didn't coincide with my schedule, so I sent him alternative dates. He replied by cable: "I'm happy to put you up. Driver will meet you at airport and bring you to me. Saul."

When I got to Almería, I saw a driver holding an envelope: "Sta. [sic] Harriet Wasserman," it read, in Saul's hand. The abbreviation was for "Santa"—Saint. The enclosed note read: "Dear Harriet. Your driver Juan who speaks no English will take you to the home of Barley Alison where you'll be her guest. My maid is too messy. I'll meet you at Barley's house at one o'clock and then we can go for a swim. Saul."

What? Stay at the house of someone I never met? I went straight to the counter. It was dawn on Sunday morning. "When does the next plane leave for Barcelona?"

"On Thursday."

Alone in the backseat during the ride to Casa Alison, I felt the way I had when I was eight years old and sent to a godforsaken summer camp in New Jersey. We finally got to the coast and went up very narrow roads with hairpin turns, up and up and up, and then, at the top of the mountain, there was Barley Alison, looking just as Saul described her: like a female rooster. In her sixties, she was extremely thin, flat front and back, with baguette-type legs and long white hair piled in a bun on top of her head. She had small features, a beautiful little nose, pretty blue eyes, and a cigarette in her mouth, with bits of ash dropping off. She was a chain-smoker.

I stumbled out of the car, handed her the champagne I had brought for Saul, and muttered apologies for intruding. Addressing me in a very exaggerated British accent, she exposed a pronounced, nicotine-stained overbite, in quite jarring contrast to her fine features: "No, no! Not-ta-tall. María will show you to your room. María!"

So there was María, twelve years old, who had been her maid since age eight—no child labor laws—carrying my bags into this glorious room in sun-splashed whites, its arched windows looking down into the sea.

"If you want to take a sh-aah'r [shower]," Barley informed me in that deep smoker's voice and almost incomprehensible accent, "let me tell you my mother is down the hall. She's a bit dotty. She walks around naked and has a hacking cough. Sounds worse than it is."

Within an hour and a half of my arrival, I was sitting on a chair on the veranda, overlooking the Mediterranean. Barley had called me down from my room when Saul arrived to pick me up for lunch. I had been lying on the bed and staring at the ceiling, wondering: what next.

Saul was sitting flanked by Barley and her other house-guests. All had drinks in hand, Barley a cigarette in her free hand. They were in a semicircle. I sat across from them. David Farrer, a senior editor from Secker & Warburg, then Saul, and Charles Lattimer and Michel Bloch, "a male married homosexual couple," Barley had informed me earlier. Michel, a rather well known European concert pianist and recording artist, was the spitting image of Harpo Marx, curly red hair and all.

Saul hadn't risen to greet me. I noticed he was deeply tanned. "What's new in New York?" was the first question he put to me. Before I could answer, Barley piped up. "Well, we're all going to convince Harriet to stay, even though Saul is leaving tomorrow." Everyone looked embarrassed, obviously they already knew the big news.

I turned to Saul, who was gazing at the tile floor, and asked, "Is that true?"

Without looking at me, he nodded his head.

I turned my head to stare at the sea, stunned. Well, I

thought to myself, here I am. There's nothing I can do except let go.

On the drive to Saul's place for lunch, just the two of us, he asked somewhat sheepishly, "Are you sore at me? This is good for you. You're not social enough."

Though blowing my stack at the outrageous predicament, I certainly didn't want to let him know. I don't think I did an absolutely convincing job, though. There was a little tension in the air, and I was silent the rest of the twenty minutes to Casa Pillet.

When we got there, a picnic table was already set. We didn't even go inside. Saul and I sat down, and as soon as we did, his maid, who was about thirteen, brought out hot Spanish omelettes, and Saul served red wine. It was my impression that he was still a little uncomfortable and wary. "I hope you don't mind staying at Barley's. She'll love to have you."

The main subject of the luncheon was a writer whom Saul had encouraged me to take on as a client. Her contract had been negotiated at Viking earlier in the year. The author was particularly high-strung and difficult. Unfortunately, there had been a misunderstanding as to whether the manuscript was fiction or nonfiction. The editor had understood Saul to describe the work as a novel, and when Saul then called me that same Saturday afternoon, I too understood it to be a novel. Fortunately for me, I did not have occasion to refer to the nature of the work; unfortunately for the editor, he had accepted the novel in a letter, thus causing much *Sturm und Drang*. The author complained bitterly to Saul and then phoned me in a rage.

For self-protection, I had to keep my mouth shut, even when the beleaguered editor pleaded, "I would *swear* that Saul said *novel*." I knew Saul had, because he had called it that to me. I felt guilty that I couldn't validate the editor's reality. To have confessed to him would have made his situation no better, only mine worse.

Saul asked again, "Why did they take it if they thought it was a novel?"

"You have tremendous power over Viking. If you suggest it, they'll take it. They can't say no to you."

But Saul didn't get it. At the time, Viking had been his publisher since 1948, more than twenty-five years.

For dessert, Saul had an open and partially eaten chocolate bar. He offered me a piece, which I declined. Breaking off and eating a piece himself, he then called the maid out. "I'm going to give this to her. She likes something sweet." He gave the girl the chocolate bar wrapper with the bit that was left.

"A treat for you."

"*Gracias, Señor*."

And then we were off, around those hairpin turns once more, to drop me at my new home away from home. At Barley's, he asked me if I wanted to go for a swim, but I didn't.

I found out that the date I had given him for my arrival came a day after his previous houseguest (and future wife), Alexandra Ionescu Tuleca, a Romanian mathematician, had visited. Saul and Alexandra had met at a Northwestern University faculty party.

Alexandra: "I haven't read any of your books."

Saul: "Neither have I read any of yours. Who's your publisher?"

"Springer Verlag."

"What's the title?"

"*Topics in the Theory of Lifting.*"

They both laughed, and that was the beginning of their romance.

Saul had invited Alexandra to Almería to meet Barley and to have Barley check her out. He depended on Barley. She was British, and he thought she had class. Advising him on his courtship was one of the zillion things she did for Saul. She'd shop with and for him. He relied on her taste in fabrics, china, linens, crystal, silver. Barley, who was Saul's age, never married, lived vicariously through all Saul's courtships, and became very friendly with all of his mistresses, ex-mistresses, and wives. She kept saying, "Saul, Alexandra's European. She's absolutely wonderful." He always told me it was Barley who convinced him to marry her. That summer, she was giving him specific lessons on how to court a European lady. Obviously, a European lady would not want another woman staying in her intended's house. I guess he knew I wouldn't have come if he had told me I'd be a stranger's guest.

The next morning, before Saul's departure for Madrid, while we were all in the tiny town at the foot of the mountain, shopping with Barley, Saul asked me to step aside and come to the bank with him.

"I don't have enough cash. Could you cash your traveler's checks for me? When you get to Barcelona, you can see Plaza y Janes and tell them I said they should advance you against my next earnings."

I knew full well that house hadn't been Saul's Spanish publisher for many years. He didn't know that. He doesn't follow business. With a few important exceptions, he doesn't know who his European publishers are, let alone the local subagents. I cashed my traveler's checks, as he asked. (In Barcelona, my client Fernando Krahn kindly took a personal check from me, and when I stopped in

London, our English co-agent advanced me the balance against Saul's earnings.)

Barley and the others went back to her house after shopping. Saul and I drove to Casa Pillet, where he was to pack his suitcase and change his clothes before coming back to Barley's to be picked up by a limo driver and taken to the airport.

In his bedroom there were piles of *Humboldt's Gift* manuscript pages: in holograph in notebooks and on loose sheets, some typed up on loose sheets with holograph changes. There hadn't even been time enough to discuss his progress. "See, I've been working," Saul said. As he was packing, he handed me a batch of pages and a lined spiral notebook. "Here, take these. You can use them as a tax deduction."

He also decided not to pack an old red, white, and green knit Italian sport shirt and a jockstrap—both of which he offered to autograph and give to me.

I accepted the shirt without the autograph.

I ended up staying three full days after Saul's departure. Everybody was friendly and sympathetic, and I got into the routine. We breakfasted together, we went to the beach, we had lunch, dinner, drinks. The first night, I rose to clear the table after dinner; Barley was appalled. Used plates, filled ashtrays, everything was left for María. A totally unrealistic experience for me, so used to working for my living. One more day, and I think I would never have left!

Barley was a truly generous hostess. And the most work done during the day at Almería was by the men, who, after discussion, would drag her rubber raft to the beach and inflate it for the sea, on which it never bobbed. Barley chose to stretch out next to it, sunbathing while the others swam. Often she kept me by her side, wanting to talk.

My first day back at the office, I realized I had been given a sharp and pointed lesson—way beyond Barley's looking me over. After decades at the London publisher Weidenfeld & Nicolson, Barley had recently changed firms, to Secker & Warburg. I was greeted on my return to New York with an enraged letter from Sir (now Lord) George Weidenfeld. Barley had written to him that I had come to Almería to discuss moving Saul from Weidenfeld! The trip to Almería had been a setup. But I took the hint. Saul's way of making his will known is reflected in one of his favorite jokes: "Let's you and him fight." Now I knew what he wanted. I was the one who strong-armed him to leave Weidenfeld and move to Secker.

There was another specific reason for Saul's inviting me to Almería. In the words of Barley's stepmother, who arrived from the isle of Jersey early on the day Saul left, looking just like Noël Coward in drag, "Hello! I said to myself. Hello! Something odd going on here!"

Saul wanted Barley to check me out as an agent, just as she had checked out Alexandra as a wife! Luckily, I didn't piece that together until after Barley and her other house-guests, now my good friends, stood on a line on the top of the hill waving good-bye, as I, waving back, was driven to the airport. I was allowed my idyllic, unself-conscious experience of *la buena vida*—and, much younger than them all, my last summer of naïveté.

That September, Barley called to tell me that Saul had married his fourth wife. I called him: You got married? Yeah, what about it?

Then, in December of that year, Saul won a fiction prize from *Playboy*, for an excerpt from *Humboldt's Gift*. There was a luncheon at the Waldorf-Astoria, and his new wife came with him.

Alexandra was wearing a red tailored suit and appeared to be reserved and shy, very formal and European-look-ing. Her hair was up in a French twist. You could tell that she wasn't an American because she carried a pocketbook with a handle in the crook of her arm, in an old-fash-ioned style, just above her wrist. She reminded me, in a way, of what I thought my mother may have been like in the forties, very Eastern European immigrant, elegant. There was something about her face. Saul took her elbow. She was gracious. I sat at her table. She hardly spoke.

I came to find out later that the shy, faraway look came from being so taken up by mathematics. I got to know Alexandra quite well when I visited them in Vermont. She would start the day by going into her studio with her mathematics, then she would come downstairs to make lunch, and it would take her a while to make the transition from higher mathematics to reality. One day, she had just come down from her studio and was making hamburgers, and as she was pressing them into the grill she kept muttering, "Yup, yup, yup, yup, yup, yup." I was watching her and smiling, and she became conscious that she was doing this. "Harriet, do you speak to yourself too?" she said. Then I started laughing at her idea that speaking to herself was "Yup, yup, yup, yup, yup, yup." And that's when she told me that her mind is so caught up in the mathematical thing that it takes her a while to unwind.

Saul was still working on *Humboldt's Gift*. When it was just about completed, he and Alexandra and I were having lunch at Lutèce. Saul asked, "What about those pages?"

I felt very strongly about the scene in which a character who is very much attached to the hero, Charlie, commits suicide. The character had been filled with religious conviction:

"She knew three thousand Bible verses. Brought up on hellfire and damnation . . ."

"Her Christianity was the delirious kind. She moaned in her sleep . . . 'I know there is a hell. There is a hell—there is!'"

I figured that it would be almost unthinkable for this character to commit suicide, against her nature and her fear of hell. It would have to mean that there's a lot of bad stuff Charlie wasn't telling us.

I gave Saul my honest response, told him an accident would be better.

He gave me a piercing, skeptical look and didn't say anything, but in the next draft, the character was lost in a plane crash in South America. I smiled to myself. It was a validation. It validated to me that my reaction was okay. It validated that whenever I had a strong reaction to a work, I had to express it.

(Some years later, a writer came to see if I would be her agent. At the end of the meeting, she said, "By the way, tell Saul I owe him, because thanks to him I sold my apartment on Riverside Drive for top dollar. A couple walked in to see it, and the woman said, 'I was Saul Bellow's mistress for many years. I'm Demmie Vonghel in

Humboldt's Gift.' Her husband was silent, grinning and as proud as Punch. She wanted the apartment, and I knew that I'd get top dollar. Not only was she buying the quintessential Bellovian Upper West Side apartment: She was buying the ghost of Saul Bellow.")

Humboldt's Gift was published in August 1975 and became a world best-seller. Reprinted by Avon, it was Saul's hugest paperback best-seller to date. Peter Mayer at Avon also bought all available backlist titles when the licenses expired.

I received a phone call from the Associated Press in May to confirm a quote: "In Humboldt's Gift, does Saul Bellow say, 'The Pulitzer Prize is for the birds—for the pullets?'"

"Yes."

"Well, Humboldt's Gift just won the Pulitzer." My caller asked for Saul's number. When I phoned Saul later, I told him the quote would be used on the wires and in the papers. He was greatly amused.

Saul turned sixty that year, and I threw a surprise birthday banquet for him. It was to follow a cocktail party in my apartment, which would allow his friends to meet Alexandra and permit mathematician friends of hers who lived in New York to meet her new spouse. And I would get the chance to know Alexandra better.

Saul suffers from Seasonal Affective Disorder. A man

who needs sunshine in his life, he can get as cloudy as a cloudy day. He must have a patch of chlorophyll on his chest, is the way he puts it. I've seen his moods as balmy as a spring day and as fierce as a summer squall. Approaching birthdays, particularly significant ones, can set him off as well. His birthday is June 10 (though some calendars list it as a month later), and the cocktail party was on the ninth; he protested we were aging him before his time.

Thirty-five people were invited over for cocktails, and the twenty who were going to the surprise dinner party afterward were handed little slips with the time and place. When I had called Alexandra to discuss a surprise party, she wasn't sure it was a good idea. "Oh, I don't think he will like surprises." I said I'd take the responsibility.

The maître d' at the Shun Lee on Second Avenue and Forty-eighth Street, with whom I discussed plans, told me sixty was a very big birthday in China. A person gains wisdom by that year. "Very big birthday. Very big." We arranged to curtain off a corner of the restaurant.

Saul's friend Herb McCloskey lived around the corner, and it was Herb who, after cocktails, would suggest, "Let's go to a Chinese restaurant."

The cocktail party went well. People didn't seem to want to leave. Philip Roth, Saul's friend and former student, came with friend, editor, and publisher Aaron Asher. Saul Steinberg, the artist, was there, and Tom Victor, the photographer. John Cheever and his wife, Mary, had brought along their daughter, Susan; she walked in right past me and never said a word. She came to the dinner as well.

John and Saul were in an intense conversation, when Saul excused himself to "go to the can."

It was getting late, and in his absence, most everyone invited to the dinner left.

Saul came back. "Where's John? I can't believe it. I don't see John for years, I go to take a leak, and he's gone." Saul is all depressed. Herb says, "Oh, Saul, come on. We'll go to a Chinese restaurant by my apartment."

"No, I don't feel like eating. I'm not hungry. I had plenty of food here. I can't believe it. We didn't even finish the conversation."

By the time I get to the restaurant, twenty guests are seated behind the curtain. I tell the maître d' there will be four more. "No way. No room. No room." I have to fix this quick. The table is in the shape of a square U. I grab four chairs and bring them over. Everyone would have to squeeze together tightly. "How waiters go?" From the inside, I explain. Instead of serving from the outside, they can walk into the middle and serve.

Saul walked in. "Surprise!!!" and a chorus of "Happy Birthday."

He *was* surprised. Herb said he'd had a hard time getting Saul to come, he was so depressed. Saul took a look at John and threw his head back and laughed.

Saul sat at the closed end of the U, with Alexandra between him and Philip Roth. He was irritated about a piece Philip had written for the *Village Voice*, in which he involved Saul. (In that same issue there was an ad on the personals page: "Herzog Seeking His Ramona.") Philip leaned behind Alexandra and said, "I don't mean to talk behind your wife's back, but . . ."

In fact, that year Philip dedicated a collection of essays, entitled *Reading Myself and Others*, "To Saul Bellow, the 'other' I have read from the beginning, with the deepest pleasure and admiration."

Nature called: John Cheever had to go to the bathroom. Everyone was so squeezed in—and bubbly—there was no way out except to go beneath the table and emerge from under the white cloth. Saul said, "This is just like birth—a tight situation." The rest of the night, people were sliding under the table and emerging from the white, almost-floor-length cloth. It was very jolly.

P.S. Son Adam's commencement from Dalton School that weekend was the primary reason Saul had come to town. On Monday, Saul asked me to accompany Adam to buy a brand-new typewriter, a high school graduation present from his father, advancing the price against future earnings. We went to the Lexington Typewriter Shop, and Adam made his choice after trying a number of models. As we were leaving, I leaned over a machine to see what Adam had typed (I figured on "Now is the time for all good men to come to the aid of their country"). The line read:

"My name is Moses Herzog."*

Saul often popped into my office unannounced when he came to town. One fall day, he blew into the office, and I walked him to Grand Central. He was on his way to an appointment, before leaving for Israel. We were early; his train was in the station.

"Let's go in the smoking car. Ever since I quit, I love to inhale and remember what it was like."

He told me he was afraid of Alexandra because of her temper.

"Look," I said, "lots of things that get off to a shaky start become very solid. Calm down, give it a chance."

---

*The first line of the novel itself reads: "If I'm out of my mind, it's all right with me, thought Moses Herzog."

In Jerusalem, he and Alexandra went to the national artists' colony, Mishkenot Sha-ananim.

Saul wrote me from Israel that things were okay. He said he would sit and write at a window with bars; passersby looked in on him as though he were a lion in the zoo, and sometimes he'd stretch and lick his paws.

We corresponded. I spoke to him frequently, phoning him in the dining room. Once, my call came during the dinner hour: He'd been sitting next to Abba Eban, who was eating boiled chicken and mashed potatoes with gravy. Everything seemed to be fine.

In Jerusalem, Saul kept a journal in a ledger book. When he got home, he asked me to sell the journal of his trip as an article to *Harper's*. He urged that it be done quickly, as it was timely. An agent serves two purposes, side by side: one, to act as first professional reader; and two, to take care of all the business and let a writer be completely free to do what only he or she can do— which is write.

I told Saul his account *was* timely, but it was also time-less and should be a book. Monthly periodicals, I explained, have at least a three-to-four month lead time. What I should do is take the manuscript to Tom Guinzburg, son of the late Harold, at Viking and let him offer on the book, and to Rachel MacKenzie at *The New*

*Yorker* (a weekly would publish sooner) for first serial rights. The book would be beautifully edited, copyedited, and fact-checked by *The New Yorker* and could come out fast. That's what we did. I suggested a change in the title for his first book-length work of nonfiction, which he liked: *To Jerusalem and Back: A Personal Account.*

# III.

## Nobel Savage

*S*aul and Alexandra were having breakfast in their South Side apartment in Chicago on Tuesday, October 19, 1976. They were in the midst of packing to move into Alexandra's newly expanded North Side apartment on Thursday. I called. "How are you doing?" I asked Saul.

"Alexandra and I were just about to split . . . an English muffin together."

"Have you heard anything new?" I asked him (a question he invariably asked me when he called).

"No. Have you?"

"As a matter of fact, I have. I just had a top-secret call from Stockholm. Word's leaked out. Saul Bellow is to be the Nobel Prize laureate in literature for 1976. The official announcement will be made one P.M. Swedish time Thursday."

"Oh, boy. Can I tell my wife?"

"Yes."

"Excuse me. I have to go to the can."

It had been our Swedish agent who called to report the leak. A TV news station in Stockholm had called Bonnier's, Saul's publisher, to ask for biographical data and photos of Saul Bellow. The prize is always announced at one o'clock Swedish time on a Thursday. It is never, *ever*, leaked.

Yet by later that afternoon I was getting calls from Rome, from everywhere. By then the Swedish Academy realized what had happened. They're very protective and secretive. It was possible that they might even change their decision and not award a prize for literature that year. Saul got a cable from a Swedish journalist friend, congratulating him, and then the journalist sent him another, telling Saul he'd better disregard the earlier cable for now.

On Wednesday, CBS-TV called and said they wanted to send a film crew to Chicago, just in case an official announcement was made. I told CBS Saul was moving on Thursday.

"Better yet." From where to where was he moving? They'd send crews to both places. I wasn't about to give out the information, it was the last thing Saul would want.

All that commotion. Saul laughed. "If I don't get the prize tomorrow, it will be the funniest thing that ever happened to me."

Late in the day, I got a triumphant call from CBS. The writer Richard Stern, Saul's old friend from the University of Chicago, had given out the addresses.

I called Saul very early Thursday morning, about a half hour before the prize would be announced. He was expecting the movers, he had classes that day. "I'm under the covers with Jane Austen, and I'm going to stay with Jane Austen until it's all over."

(*Carpe diem.* Who shows up at the apartment? Richard Stern, with a bottle of champagne. Four weeks later, an article by him appeared in *The New York Times Magazine*: "Bellow's Gift." "How many American authors have published first-rate imaginative books over a thirty-year period? Perhaps three, Henry James, Faulkner and now Bellow.")

I heard it was official from the music director at WNCN-FM, as it came over the station's wire, at almost the same time and called. In between busy signals, we connected, and I offered my congratulations with a quote, adapted for the occasion and from memory, from an old Russian novelist, V. V. Rozanov, with which Saul had concluded his 1973 Smithsonian Lecture, entitled "Literature in the Age of Technology":

"A million years passed before my soul was let out into the technological world. That world was filled with ultra-intelligent machines, but the soul, after all, was a soul, and it had waited a million years for its turn and did not intend to be cheated of its birthright by a lot of mere gimmicks. It had come from the far reaches of the universe and it was interested but not overawed."

The news was on all the networks that night: press conferences, footage of Chicago, Lake Shore Drive, the university, Himself.

Sixteen members of the Bellow family attended the ceremonies in Sweden, an unprecedented number that made front-page news in the Stockholm papers: wife Alexandra; sister Jane; brother Sam and sister-in-law Nina; sons Gregory, Adam, and Daniel; niece Lesha, her husband, and their three daughters; mother-in-law Dr. Floria Bagdasar; her sister with her daughter and son-in-law.

All the Bellows came to London first. Barley Alison—now Saul's British publisher, with her own imprint, The

Alison Press, at Secker & Warburg—gave an elegant sit-down dinner in her South Kensington house. The immediate family attended, as well as English literati. The rest of the Bellows came for coffee and dessert. Saul and Alexandra left for Stockholm a day earlier than the entourage.

I sat next to Saul's sister Jane on the flight from London to Stockholm and the even longer taxi ride from the airport to the Grand Hotel. Jane had been in Miami for the winter. On the plane she grumbled to me about having to fly to freezing Chicago from Florida to get her mink coat out of storage, and she told me that having to collect it weighed heavily in her decision. For a long while, she didn't know if she'd come or not. It was a big schlepp. I liked her from that first meeting. We've been friendly ever since.

At that time, Saul's eldest son, Greg, who lived in California, was a psychiatric social worker in his thirties; his middle child, Adam, the spitting image of his father, was nineteen; and his youngest, Daniel, was twelve. The boys all had different mothers and, to some extent, a different father as well.

Once, on one of Greg's rare trips to New York, our first real meeting, I invited him to lunch at the Algonquin. He told me, "I watched my father on TV! My father, awarded a Nobel Prize! You see, we were living in Forest Hills and he was just my father, he wasn't famous. I was nine years old. The worst thing that happened was that my parents got divorced. I was so ashamed. I was the only kid in school whose parents were divorced."

Anita, Saul's first wife, Greg's mother, was a social worker who looked, I was told, just like Simone Signoret. Saul went through a period of Reichian therapy during their marriage and was told that Anita was too conventional and was holding him back. They divorced. She moved to California with Greg and remarried.

Saul was still not famous when he married his second wife, Sandra, and when Adam was born. (In a postcard to Henry Volkening on Adam's birth date, in 1957, Saul wrote, "Adam arrived today looking wrinkled and red and tired and as though he walked all the way.") Adam was very young when his parents were divorced, but by 1963 divorce wasn't as shocking.

Saul married Susan, and Daniel was born in 1964. *Herzog* had become a huge commercial success. Saul Bellow was a household name, not only a famous writer but a real celebrity. Daniel's father and mother split when he was four. Saul's divorce from Susan involved alimony suits, fraud suits, etc., lasting a good twenty and more years. I visited Saul one afternoon of a particularly grueling courtroom session in 1971. He looked wiped out. "I watch her, and as a character in a novel she's delicious, but in real life she's a monster."

I got caught in the fallout.

I wasn't brash enough to be an agent, I should wear funny hats like Marianne Moore or something. Then Saul said, "Your father's a doctor! And so is Susan's." No comparison, I said. My father's an old-fashioned Lower East Side general practitioner. He walks around, his pockets bulging with singles, because he charges his patients one or two dollars, at the most, and more often gives them samples and treats them for free. I may have been a doctor's daughter, but I was never a princess.

It was a very bitter breakup from the beginning. Father and Mother would communicate through young Daniel. From an early age, he had to learn to play them to stay alive. He was right in the middle. As a youth, Daniel suffered from a bad case of asthma, perhaps because he came into a world of such enmity between his parents.

Whenever Saul was in New York, he met Daniel in my office. He'd be anticipating the meeting. I remember him waiting in the dark (Saul hates fluorescent lights and had me turn them off). Once, Daniel came running in and jumped on him—he often did that—and grabbed his neck. "Pop! Pop!" Saul hugged him back. Thirty seconds later, he put him down. He looked at Daniel, deflated "Oh, God, you have the Glassman nose." Right away, Daniel deflated too.

But in Stockholm, father and sons were celebrating with the extended family. Adam (then in his late teens, now the editorial director of The Free Press) had had T-shirts printed up as gifts to his family upon the announcement of the Nobel Prize, they read "Nobel Savage," a pun on the award and on the name of a great literary magazine, *Noble Savage*,* which Saul edited in the early sixties. *Noble Savage* ran for five issues and attracted an unrivaled number and quality of writers and contributions.

Stockholm's Grand Hotel, on the Grand Canal, was right out of a Sonja Henie movie. It was snowing heavily, everywhere were smiling faces, a cheerful and excited feeling, bustle, bustle, bustle, and celebration.

The Nobel ceremony took place late in the afternoon. It gets dark very early in Stockholm. By four it's absolute nighttime. Saul's American publisher, Thomas Guinzburg, and I were driven to the ceremony at the Royal Opera House in the car of his Swedish publisher, Gerard Bonnier. Saul's brother and sister-in-law were escorted on foot,

---

* "I am as free as Nature first made man, 'Ere the base laws of servitude began / When wild in woods the noble savage ran."—John Dryden, "The Conquest of Granada."

though it was snowing. They walked to the opera house from the Grand Hotel because it was the Sabbath and they weren't allowed to ride after sundown. Earlier that day, they had made a trial walk to be sure the distance wasn't too long.

The ceremony itself was quite something: Musicians in eighteenth-century costumes, with wigs and trumpets, sounded fanfares as the laureates marched onto the Royal Opera stage and took their seats. Behind them, against the back wall, mezzanine level, was a full orchestra, which struck up a medley from *West Side Story*, starting on the downbeat with "When you're a Jet, you're a Jet all the Way." That was the year all Americans and only Americans won Nobel Prizes.

Saul and Milton Friedman, laureate in economics, sat next to each other on the stage in the first row. Saul leaned over to whisper something to Friedman that made him laugh. Afterward, I asked what he'd said. He had just paraphrased a Wordsworth poem: "Milton! thou shouldst be living at this hour: England hath need of thee."

During the ceremony, students rose up from the audience, shouted, and pulled out a banner, very anti-Chile and very anti-Friedman. A prize in economics wasn't intended by Alfred Nobel but in recent years had been added by the Academy. Nobel, the inventor of dynamite, excluded a mathematics prize because his wife had an affair with and left him for a mathematician. Literature, medicine and physiology, chemistry, physics, and peace, were part of the original endowment.

In my opinion, the Nobel Prize is one of the most brilliant PR jobs in almost two thousand years, and the Nobel Academy is unrivaled for its investment skills. The Academy is made up of eleven Swedish men, but the prize is deemed, worldwide, as if bestowed by the Divine on the Highest.

I've noticed that there are always articles on the deserving people who didn't get the Nobel Prize in literature. I've never seen it done in any other category. Who should have gotten it, who shouldn't, all the great writers who didn't. Actually, it's just a decision, a very subjective one really, of eleven Swedish men who have to agree unanimously on a winner for the year. That's it. Graham Greene was often shortlisted, but he couldn't get a unanimous decision. And as I understand it, with Saul Bellow, the same: shortlisted many times, but in his case there were two members of the eleven-member panel who year after year would not swing their votes. It came to pass that one member died and was replaced by someone favorably disposed to Saul. Then the other holdout died. "Oh, you mean it only took two men to die for me to get the Nobel Prize!"

The Nobel Prize banquet, held at the town hall, fol-

lowed the ceremony at the opera house. Both were tele-
vised live.

To help celebrate, Saul's eldest brother, Sam, had
received a top-secret dispensation from entering federal
prison for pharmaceutical kickbacks at his nursing
homes. (Saul: "He has to come now? He has to do this to
me?") Brother Sam told everybody that he and his wife,
Nina, were on their way to their condo in Tel Aviv. At the
banquet, Nina even tried to convince Tom Guinzburg
(who was flanked by the couple at the table) to buy a
condo next to theirs. Brother Morris wasn't there; he was
on the outs with the entire family, including his own son.

Before the dinner, there were many "Skoal"s—nonstop
toasts at which everybody rose and drank. Twelve-year-
old Daniel was toasting with the rest of us and beginning
to glow with the excitement and the wine. He was in tails
and white tie and wore the white-cloth lapel button that
distinguished the laureates' children. What a time he was
having!

I spent a lot of time keeping an eye on Daniel. He
played "fall down" in the center of the lobby of the Grand
Hotel with the children of Barry Blumberg, the co-winner in medicine. They were asked by the staff, the bell
captain, and the concierge to pipe down. We went for a
romp in the snowy streets of the Old Town. I bought him

some chocolate (five dollars for a candy bar!). Daniel and I became good buddies. In Sweden, this was one happy kid.

Radiating from one long table down the center of the enormous hall, where the King and Queen and the laureates sat, were tables for the guests. A waiter stood in front of the table, each waiter's eyes on the headwaiter standing on the marble staircase that led down from the front balcony. At his signal, in unison, each of the tables were served—but not before the King and Queen and the laureates were served. There were at least a thousand people to be fed. The first course arrived: a little crescent pastry with a tiny *quenelle*. Then another dish, an orange stuffed with something. Greg, at my left, said, "I'm going to wait for the meat dish."

The next thing we knew, all the lights went down, and a spotlight was shone on the balcony, where each of the waiters held a silver tray bearing a Baked Alaska, a huge letter N and a candle in the center. All marched down to music. It struck me as being very American for an "Old World" catered affair. Greg had Baked Alaska for dinner.

At the end of the banquet, a page in eighteenth-century costume called out: "Pray silence for . . ." and he named a laureate, who came forward and made a short speech, three to five minutes. Saul's remarks were thrilling and were subsequently reprinted as an introduction, together with his formal Nobel Lecture, in a signed, deluxe limited edition. He said the child in him—for despite appearances there was a child—was delighted, but the adult skeptical. Before each laureate spoke, we'd rise and toast him. The speeches were followed by a musical interlude. Nicolai Gedda, the Metropolitan Opera tenor, sang a Sigmund Romberg solo: "Overhead the moon is beaming . . ." Then, with an all-male university chorus, he sang "Funiculi-Funiculà" (in Swedish, which broke me up).

At the ball immediately following the banquet, Daniel, flushed and very jolly, rushed up to his father between dances, placed his girlfriend's purse in one hand and her carnation in the other, and said, "Hold these." Saul shrugged his shoulders as if to say: What can I do? He stood on the sidelines while Daniel and his partner danced away. It was Daniel's mother, by the way, who collected all of Saul's Nobel Prize money.

Carl Gajdusek, the co-winner in medicine, brought along eight adopted sons wearing tails, with white lapel buttons, stack-heeled shoes, and stunned expressions. They came directly from New Guinea, where Carl had been doing his research, and they all slept in sleeping bags on the floor of his Grand Hotel room. They were completely unworldly, utterly unsophisticated. The Greenguses—Saul's niece Lesha, her husband, Sam, and their three young daughters, Dina, Rachel, and Judy—had been seated at the table with the eight kids from New Guinea. The boys took turns dancing with the girls, to the amazement of the Greenguses and everyone else.

Saul came up to me. The ballroom was popping with flashbulbs as photographers followed his every move. I thought he was going to ask me to dance, and I was debating if I wanted to in the midst of all that glare. "Harriet, can you . . . type? I need you in my suite at nine-thirty tomorrow morning. They're coming to pick up my speech at noon."

When I arrived at his suite the next morning, Saul was pale. He led me to the huge typewriter the hotel had provided. I had never used that type of machine before and had to put a couple of sofa cushions on my chair so I could reach the keyboard. I had no script to look at. Saul was reading from his notes, revising as he spoke. At the same time, he was watching my face to see my reaction. I was preoccupied, intensely listening to and then visualizing his words in order to type copy that would be good enough to give to the press. For example, he dictated, "Perhaps this is connected to the wonderful French saying

'*S'il y a un caractère, il est mauvais.*'" I closed my eyes to visual-
ize and comprehend, my stomach in knots as it used to be
while taking the *dictée* part of French final exams in high
school. Saul, who was watching me intently, would say,
"What's wrong? Don't you like it?" Or at another passage,
while I was concentrating mightily and typing as fast as I
could: "Oh, that wasn't funny? You didn't think that was
funny?" He was crestfallen. "Oh, yeah, yeah, that was
funny." This went on for two and a half hours.

Saul was under great tension, writing the lecture
overnight, revising as he went along, and gauging my
reaction. He had decided against the other option available to him: returning to Stockholm four to six weeks
later to deliver his lecture. I suspect he wanted to get it
over with and was at the same time thinking something
like, Oh my God, I'm writing a Nobel speech, me, this
kid from Chicago. That's the way he is. For instance, he
usually doesn't say, "I'm writing a novel." He'll start, "I'm
writing a short story," then "a long short story,"
then: "I'm writing a novella." Then it looks as though it
may be a novel.

Dictating to me, he quoted a lot from Robbe-Grillet
and others, which I noticed he does when he's not writing
fiction.

While Rachel MacKenzie was editing *To Jerusalem and*

Back for The New Yorker, she called and asked me why Saul constantly quoted others in this fact piece. We both agreed: He's the original thinker, it's what he has to say that people want to hear. Rachel asked me what she should do. "Just tell him." Which she did, and he deleted a lot of the quotes. People who don't know Saul well usually think he's very self-possessed, very self-assured. But for Saul, every book is his first book, and he is always the first-time writer welcoming reinforcement.

If we'd had more time, if the press hadn't been coming to pick up the speech at noon, I would have reminded Saul of what Rachel had said: "Why are you quoting so much? You're the original thinker. You're the one people want to hear."

When he finished, he looked at me and asked what I thought. "Good," I replied.

After handing the speech to the courier, Saul and I left the suite, the ordeal, and the enormous typewriter behind us. We "sneaked" into the Wintergarden restaurant in the Grand Hotel and sat behind a sheltering column, unnoticed by anyone. From where we sat, we had a full view of the big buffet table. We watched Daniel take a plate, sniff each dish of food as he went around. Saul laughed. "He has to watch out for crustaceans. He's allergic."

The young orchestra members across the room, in Père

Noël hats and other Christmas attire, spotted Saul and broke into a rendition of "Chicago, Chicago, that toddling town." He waved to them. "Now, this part I really like."

Next day, before Saul delivered his speech at the Stock Exchange, Gerard Bonnier hosted a luncheon in Saul's honor at his country home, attended by U.S., British, German, and other European publishers. The house had lofty raftered ceilings throughout and, in the dining room, oil portraits of the numerous Nobel Prize winners Bonnier published. The portraits hung all around the room—even on the beams. There were four round tables, with ten guests at each. I was sitting with Alexandra, who was quite happy, composed, and elegant. One of Saul's sons sat at each of the remaining three tables.

At the end of the luncheon, Bonnier gave a short speech, offered a toast, and sat down. Daniel clinked his glass with his fork. When he had gotten everyone's attention, he said: "I'd just like to say my father has been so busy, but he still had time for me. Thanks, Pop."

Up stood Greg, who was at his father's table. "My young brother has given me the courage to say something I've always wanted to say."

Greg's voice was cracking. Alexandra put her elbows on the table and her face in her hands. Adam was at the table across from Saul's. He didn't blink. He didn't move. I looked at both of them, Adam and Saul, they were absolutely fixed and still.

Greg was standing there, his walrus mustache trembling slightly. "I never thought you loved me, and I never understood what the creative process was. You were behind a closed door all the time, writing, listening to Mozart." He was looking straight at his father. "I was young. I didn't know what you were doing behind the closed door. I didn't understand the creative process."

All the European publishers, all of them men, were sitting very stiff and upright. They could have had rods up their spines. Looks of total shock—horror almost—on their faces. They'd never seen a father and son like this before, and you could sense them experiencing a vicarious pain and embarrassment at this public display.

"And then . . ." Greg was barely controlling himself. "And then I had my own child. I witnessed the birth of my own child and then I understood what the creative process was, and I understood then that you really did love me."

No one moved. All eyes turned away. Greg sat down, and after a stunned silence people began to leave their tables. Saul was one of the first. He stood up quickly and went straight over to his middle child, put out his hand, and shook Adam's. "Thanks, kid, for not saying anything."

And off he went, in a stretch limo, entourage at his

side, for a return to the city.

At the Stock Exchange, Jane, mink coat draped over her shoulders, dozed off as her kid brother delivered his Nobel Lecture. She was seated in the first row, smack in front of the podium, at the center of an auditorium shaped like an amphitheater. Everyone had a clear view of her nodding off, including Saul, whose sparkling water fizzed shakily into the microphone every time he caught sight of her. Greg and Adam, on either side, kept elbowing her throughout the speech.

Saul's never truly been conscious of having received the prize—in the sense that being a Nobel laureate is simply not part of his consciousness the way being a kid from Chicago is. Ushered and escorted from here to there by an aide-de-camp and an entourage, he said to me later, "My feet never touched the ground once." And that's how he sees it. To this day.

When Saul returned home, his old friend the late Sam Goldberg* asked him, "How was Stockholm?"

"Meshuga!" That's all. On to the next subject.

---

*Whom Saul first met at a Greenwich Village bookshop in 1950 and who proudly told everyone his claim to fame: "I'm Mintouchian in *The Adventures of Augie March*."

# IV.

## The Best Is Yet to Be

*A*fter thirty years at Viking, Saul's new publishers were going to be Harper & Row, and he was to sign his first contract with them in December 1978, for a novel entitled *Far Out*. Harper had prepared a luncheon for him in their dining room to celebrate. A limo would be waiting for Saul at the airport. It was a big day.

Midmorning, my assistant told me Alexandra was on the phone in Chicago, extremely upset. I picked it up. She could hardly speak. "I got a telegram . . . my mother . . . coma. Saul . . . airport . . ."

"Okay," I said. "I'll hang up right away and see if I can page him at O'Hare. I'll try to catch him. Don't worry."

Alexandra was an only child who had defected from Romania to come to Yale in 1957, all by herself. Her father had been a world-famous brain surgeon, and she was very attached to her widowed mother, formerly the country's minister of health, who lived in Bucharest. And now this awful thing: her mother stricken, in a coma in Romania, and Saul wasn't there.

I called TWA and asked that he be paged. They were just boarding. I said it was an extreme emergency, and I waited and waited and waited, and on came Saul.

"What's the matter?" I was just about to get on the plane."

"I know," and I told him what had happened.

He said, "Oh," and went straight back to their apartment.

I then called off the limo. Harper held the luncheon anyway, because all the guests were already arriving.

Winthrop Knowlton, who was then the Harper CEO, had connections in Washington. He knew an officer at the Romanian desk at the State Department, and as soon as I reported what had happened, he said he'd get in touch and see that Saul and Alexandra got a visa. Which he did. Everyone was a little afraid of

Alexandra's going back and tried to get protection for her under the U.S.

Erwin Glikes, the publisher of Harper & Row, and I ended up flying to Chicago on Saturday morning; Saul was to take off for Bucharest that night. He was very shaken up, he said we are all put together with spit and string. He signed the contract.

It was definitely not Saul's style, rushing off like that to be a support to someone. Saul knew Alexandra's mother and her aunt, whose married daughter lived in California. Both of them had gotten permission to attend the Nobel Prize ceremony. He respected his mother-in-law, who never quite approved of him.

Suddenly he was behind the Iron Curtain, in the old apartment where Alexandra had grown up. It was the back apartment of the fourth floor, and the concierge was compliments of the KGB. Saul would write in the farthest back room of the back apartment. It was freezing all the time. There were cyclamens around, bright red flowered plants that hardly ever last because they have to be at 55 degrees exactly. But they did well in that apartment, because it was always 55 degrees. He said it was brutal there, really brutal.

It's my impression that Saul was thrilled the first years of his married life with Alexandra. First of all, she was

Christian; I think he liked that. She was a mathematician, she had the Ph.D. that he didn't have, and she was well known in her special field.

He actually took a course in calculus, then decided "She's hot, and I'm lukewarm." So he dropped it. He introduced her to literature. He said once that it was great being married to somebody who couldn't speak English very well, because she hadn't heard all the old jokes. And she was elegant, distinguished, regal, well brought up, and from a prominent family.

They were in Romania for a few weeks. The government gave Alexandra a lot of trouble. At first they wouldn't let her in. Then they wouldn't let her in the hospital to see her mother. She became very, very upset.

Everything was secret and censored. Hardly anyone knew where Saul and Alexandra were, and no one could get to them. On December 11, there was a knock on the door. A courier from the American Embassy handed Saul a copy of *The New York Times*. Isaac Bashevis Singer won the Nobel Prize and had just delivered his acceptance speech in Stockholm. Singer began his address in English: "I understand when Saul Bellow gave his speech it was very long and nobody understood what he said." There's no Iron Curtain for bad news. Five months earlier, when it was announced that Singer would be the 1978 laureate in literature, Saul had sent him a congratulatory telegram in Yiddish, in which he recalled how he had translated Singer's first published story, "Gimpel the Fool," into English. He got a return note from Singer: "Yes, but one story does not make a career."

(A year or so after that, Singer spoke in Chicago. Saul attended and then went backstage. Singer said he was surprised to see him. Saul answered in Yiddish, "I didn't want you to think I was avoiding you.")

Alexandra's mother never regained consciousness, and it was clear that the end would come soon. Saul was finally allowed one visit to see his mother-in-law. When Floria first met Saul in London, on a special dispensation to leave Romania, she tried to discourage the marriage. Saul had to prove himself to her, which he really tried to do and did.

The weeks in Romania were very heavy. When her mother died, Alexandra broke down completely. She couldn't get out of bed, they had to get a doctor to give her shots. She couldn't go to the funeral. She was too sick. Extremely sick. Saul and Alexandra left Bucharest soon after her mother's death, but Alexandra needed a lot of attention. Saul had to take care of her.

The ordeal in Romania appears to have exacted its toll on their marriage.

Alexandra brought Vermont into Saul's life. Through friends of hers who helped them rent a house in 1977, they began to spend summers there. Saul decided he was a country mountain man; he absolutely loved the place.

During the summer of 1979, I spent a week in Vermont, working with Saul every morning on his novel in progress *Far Out*, which takes place in 1956 and—I quote from memory—begins something like: "It's odd how far away the fifties seem."

We worked out a schedule. Saul would dictate to me until about noon. I sat on the porch at a typing table made out of a huge wooden spool on which industrial cable is wound. Saul dictated standing up. He had already finished a typescript and was revising and editing as he dictated. He'd ask me, "Does this work?" It was exciting to be inside the process, seeing how he worked, seeing the work of art, from the inception of the thought to the polishing of it. I didn't consider it typing. When I started at Russell & Volkening, I read everything I typed. And I read everything I filed. Through that I learned a lot about the business. I try to tell my assistants that filing isn't just filing if you read what you are putting into that folder.

Alexandra, who'd been upstairs doing her math, would come down, change her shoes, and tap dance on the porch for a half hour. In the afternoon, I would proofread the pages I had typed. Sometimes Saul and Alexandra would take an excursion, sometimes they would invite me to join them. But mostly I preferred to sit under a tree and correct the pages. Usually about twenty a day. Then, in the evening, Saul would make dinner or we'd go out to eat. I was there for a full eight days, Sunday to Sunday. He was well into a revised draft.

One evening, we drove up to visit Robert Penn Warren and his wife, Eleanor Clark. "Red" Warren gave everyone an eight-ounce glass of bourbon, which I would ordinarily toss into a plant when no one was looking, but that day I drank it all. This is how the long-married couple affectionately talked to each other: Eleanor would say, "Oh, shut up, stupid!" Red ignored her and kept on talking, about FDR, about Eleanor Roosevelt, punctuated by her "Oh, shut up, stupid!" They were completely pie-eyed.

After the full glass of bourbon came two bottles of wine, lamb in some kind of cognac sauce, then strawberries with Sambuca Romana, and finally brandies. I was completely smashed. I was never so drunk in my life. And Eleanor kept saying, "Red! Red! You're going to have these people rolling under the piano. They're going to wind up in a ditch!"

We exited. Saul and Alexandra piled into the front of

the car, he in the driver's seat. Saul and I sang "Moonlight in Vermont," all the old songs, all the way back. I got up to my room. It was spinning and spinning. I could feel my liver throbbing. Around noon the next day, I could hear Saul and Alexandra through the vent from the kitchen: "I don't know where she is." There was a knock on the door. My hair was a mess, I was sweating bullets. I had thrown up on my maroon silk suit. I opened the door and said, "Saul, I'm sick." Then I heard him in the kitchen, telling Alexandra, "She's sick. She looks terrible. She's really, really sick. Maybe we should leave her alone." I was truly intoxicated, really toxic.

At four o'clock, Saul said, "Harriet, it's late, you've got to come down." I grabbed his manuscript and quickly did the trick Henry Volkening had once taught me. I memorized a couple of lines. Then I came down and said I was feeling better.

"What were you doing all day?" Saul asked.

"Reading your manuscript," in between passing out. I quoted the lines.

Even now, if I hear a word with the letters "b-o-u-r-b-o-n," I feel sick.

Saul put aside *Far Out*. Instead, out of the experience in Romania, he wrote *The Dean's December*, which was to be his first novel after the Nobel Prize. He wrote it with great spontaneity. I read it and thought it was perfect.

I came up for a long weekend in Vermont in 1980. He had written a second draft of *The Dean's December* and said, "I've put a whole new thread through it, right from the beginning." I arrived, breathless, about one o'clock Friday afternoon. Lunch was waiting for me. Saul and Alexandra had finished theirs. I ate in a hurry. Then Saul gave me the manuscript. I went up to my room to read; they went up to their room for an afternoon siesta. At about four-thirty, I heard pebbles at my window. Saul thought I had been sleeping, and he wanted to wake me up. I came downstairs and we sat outside. I told him I liked the new version a lot, but I thought the first one was perfect. He got pretty upset. "What do you mean? Don't you like it?" "Of course, but to me, the first one was perfection." "So you don't like this one then?" I was in a little bit of hot water, but that's what I really thought. I didn't think it needed to be done over again. I thought it was really great the first time: What he wanted to say, exactly the way he wanted to say it.

The next morning, about seven o'clock, there's a sharp knock on my door. It's Saul. "Harriet! Pull yourself together and come downstairs! There's something I have to say to you!"

I jumped out of bed and tried to think. I had recently

seen the film In Cold Blood, about the Clutter family. Oh my God, we're hostages; there's been a murder. That loud knock on the door and that tone of voice. Maybe one of them was sick, one of them had a heart attack in the middle of the night. I thought something terrible had happened.

When he rapped on my door he usually sang out, "O solo mio, O solo you-o!"

"Pull yourself together! There's something I have to say to you." So I pulled myself together and went down in record time.

Alexandra and Saul were dressed and in the kitchen. Alexandra was making toast and coffee. Her eyes were downcast. Surely, they'd been up since the crack of dawn.

"You know, I couldn't sleep all night. What's the big idea? I give you my revised manuscript to read, and you tell me the first one is perfect. I was up all night. What kind of thing was that?"

Alexandra agreed, quietly. "He was up all night. He was extremely upset."

At that point, the only thing I could think was: This is how you treat a guest? You knock on my door like that, scare the hell out of me.

What I said was, "I told you honestly what I thought. This version is fine, and I thought the first version was perfect."

Sometimes, when Saul revises, he loses something of the immediacy of the first version. (Not other times. He made lots of great revisions in *Humboldt's Gift*.) When he "fixes," he's telling his story again, he is repeating something to himself, and the revision becomes an attenuated version, it's immediacy and elasticity are sacrificed. This was particularly true for *The Dean's December*. I had to go very, very gingerly. The revised version is what Harper & Row published.

There was another guest that weekend. That was another thing. Me, he knocks on the door and scares me out of my wits, and in the kitchen it's: "Shh, speak lower. Warren is sleeping. You don't want to wake him up."

Saturday was very tense. I couldn't hide how I felt, and I was furious. I just couldn't speak the whole day.

For Sunday brunch, I had brought bagels and lox and cream cheese from the Second Avenue Deli—champagne too. Alexandra put the spread out, and Saul lifted his glass of champagne and made a toast to me, an effort for which I wasn't yet ready. After we finished eating I said, "I'm taking an early plane."

"But your visit was so short."

"It seemed *long* to me."

I took my bags and went straight off the porch. I heard Alexandra whisper to Saul, who was looking bewildered, "She's a little upset."

I flung my luggage in the rental car and slammed the door. Saul was standing there. He waved. I didn't roll down the window. I backed out with a real screech, spun around, and just took off.

*The Dean's December* came out the next year, and it was as if the critics were just waiting for him. The *Saturday Review* seemed to be making a fuss over the new book— a cover story and an interview. The journalist visited Saul to interview him, they got along, and then, bingo, the cover has a horrible photo of Saul and the article is called "The Greying of Saul Bellow." Saul said, "She seemed so nice when she was here." It was a ghastly, very hurtful piece. A faithful reader said to me, "Oh, I see from the *Saturday Review* that Bellow's new novel is no good."

It did get a rave from *The New York Times*, a front-page review by Robert Towers that is always quoted from: "Sentence by sentence, page by page, Saul Bellow is simply the best writer we have."

But others said it was a dark, gloomy, old man's novel. Saul is very sensitive to his reviews. The *Saturday Review* said he looked as though he could hear the bells of the winged chariot at his back door. "Old man, huh? No humor. Winged chariot. Okay, I'll show them." And he wrote *Him with His Foot in His Mouth and Other Stories*, which was lighthearted, humorous, funny, touching, and youthful. I've noticed that the subject of each new work seems often to be a reaction to the criticism of the work that came before it.

I thought that I'd be at Russell & Volkening forever. But by January '81 I knew I was being pushed out by the new owner. I asked Saul if I could call him at home after I left the office. "I'm in trouble."

Sure I could call him. "But first tell me, is it about sex or money?"

"No, it's about business."

"Oh, just business."

At home that night, I told Saul. Without missing a beat, "I'll go with you in a shot," he told me. I had first entrusted a cherished writer friend, a longtime client of R&V, who gave me a nod and added, "You are the true apostolic successor to Russell and Volkening."

On September 14, 1981, Harriet Wasserman Literary Agency was established.

One afternoon in Vermont, a couple of years earlier, Saul and I passed his huge worktable, with a whole stack of correspondence.

"You see how far behind I am? I haven't answered any of these."

"Would you like me to give you a hand?"

"Would you? That's awfully good of you."

One of the letters Saul dictated was to a new colleague of his on the Committee on Social Thought. When I handed him the letter for signature, he said: "*Ellen* Bloom? *Ellen* Bloom? It's *Allan* Bloom. Allan Bloom, political philosopher, Greek scholar, translator of *The Republic*."

The next time I heard of Allan Bloom was after my agency had been established. Bloom sent me one hundred pages of a manuscript called "American Nihilism," and I returned it, with a note saying it wasn't right for me.

A few days later, Saul called. "What's the big idea of rejecting my friend Bloom's manuscript?"

I told him I could only represent what I really loved. Not only did I not like it, but Bloom's ideas were the antithesis of mine, to put it mildly.

Saul kept saying, "I can't believe you rejected it just like that, without a word to me."

Two weeks later, my assistant announced a call from Mr. Bellow. I grabbed his call, as always. "Listen, Harriet. Allan Bloom is delighted you're going to represent his manuscript. I'm in his apartment now. Here he is."

Bloom got on the phone. He was so happy I was going to represent his work. It would be wonderful, he said. He had heard so much about me. And Saul was going to write an introduction. That was it. Bloom was so happy. For the rest of his life and two more books, he would consider me an essential part of his success. He became "An Ideal Client."

Saul and Allan became fast friends. It was Saul who sought Bloom out, knocked at his office door at the University of Chicago, introduced himself, and asked Bloom to teach a course with him in the Great Books: Dickens, Tolstoy, Stendhal, Conrad, Dostoevsky, Austen. Saul's idea was to have a dialogue in which students could get to hear the literary *and* political readings of a novel.

Mimi Sheraton, the restaurant critic, in Chicago to write a *New York Times* piece on Saul Bellow and cookery, had the rare privilege of sitting in on a class and described them as a vaudeville team. Bellow and Bloom discussed the work with each other, one from the novelist's point of view, the other from the philosopher's.

It was Bloom's intellect and, better still, his sense of humor that attracted Saul. Allan laughed heartily at Saul's jokes, quips, one-liners. Allan was the straight man.

In Chicago in 1983, Saul handed me a partial manuscript of a memoir obviously written over quite a number of years: loose pages in various stages of wear, with different typefaces, and hand-written ink comments along the margins. "I want you to take a look at this."

Back in my room at the U of C's Quadrangle Club, I had a lot of reading to do that night. "Notes of a Social Climber: In My Head It's Still 1947," by Lillian McCall, was terrific, lively, juicy, the oral history of a time, a place, and an extraordinary circle of people in the arts— W. H. Auden, Chester Kallman, Mary McCarthy, Sidney Hook, Robert Ruark, Lee Krasner, Helen Frankenthaler, Stanley Kunitz, Jackson Pollock, James Angleton, as well as a newcomer in New York, Saul Bellow.

Walking her dog in Washington Square Park early one morning, Lillian spotted the young writer.

"You're Saul Bellow, aren't you?"

"Yes, and you're not my type."

This appeared in the introduction of the original manuscript. Several drafts later, when I noticed it was gone, Lillian said, "Saul asked me to take it out."

In those days, Lillian had worked as the building's superintendent, and held an open-door salon in her living room daily, she had served in World War II as a WAC, taught psychology at New York University, and written essays on such as Freud in such as *Commentary* magazine. Inevitably, *la vie de bohème* came to an end, and people went their separate ways.

Lillian became a client, and I was thrilled to give her the news of a contract offer for the memoir on the basis of the partial manuscript Saul had given me. Lillian's daughter, Laurie, worked as a writer on *The CBS Morning News*. Upon the suggestion of a very proud Laurie, Saul appeared on a segment with Diane Sawyer and Bill Kurtis. "I'm glad to help the kid out." And he did indeed. She got a promotion.

A year later, in 1984, Lillian moved back to New York from California—where she had settled, in the 1960s— to be near her daughter and her new son-in-law and finish the manuscript. At our first meeting, Lillian, plump, with short black curly hair that stood straight up from her head, said, "You look exactly as Saul described you." (I didn't want to know any specifics.) Saul's description of Lillian to me: She looks like a Fiji Island woman. Of course, she did, right out of the cast of *South Pacific*.

A few months later, Lillian died suddenly. Her funeral service was attended by old friends from the days in Greenwich Village, none of whom had seen her in years. One of them, Toni Greenberg,* leaned over just before the service began and asked me, "Was Saul still so dependent on Lillian?" I learned that after the two of them had met in Washington Square Park all those decades ago, Saul visited Lillian and her little girl when they moved to Aspen, and they conversed every day between Sacramento, where she settled, and wherever he happened to be.

Until 1983, Saul never even mentioned her name to me!

Because I had just opened my office, I couldn't go to France when Saul was awarded the rank of Commandeur de la Légion d'honneur. He was accompanied by Alexandra, Allan Bloom, and Barley Alison. When Saul lowered his head so the President could slip the medal around his neck, he whispered in French to Mitterrand, "It's better than being hanged."

Saul told me that one morning, Allan came into their hotel room in Paris without knocking and began talking to him. Alexandra was in her slip, and after Allan had his say and left the room, she was extremely upset that Saul hadn't defended her privacy. Saul said to me, "I don't know what was bothering her. Knowing Allan, he didn't even notice." And I answered, "Precisely."

The next year's award was announced in the press. I called. "Guess who's getting the Commandeur this year?"

*The widow of Noah Greenberg, who spearheaded the revival of early music on original instruments in the U.S., founding New York Pro Musica (in whose Collegium I played recorder and krummhorn).

"Updike?"

"No."

"Günter Grass?"

No.

"Jerry Lewis."

For the first three years, my agency office was at 230 East 48th Street. Saul was genuinely excited and pleased the first time he came to see it. He handed me a box with the most beautiful Gucci scarf, flowers of every season, from crocuses to holly.* We chatted for a while, and he was beaming with pride. After all, he had a big hand in this big step in my career.

Then: "Let's go."

We walked over to Barnes & Noble, and he announced, "You have a literary agency, it needs an unabridged dictionary." We decided on the Random House, because he was listed there and I wouldn't take one without an entry for him. At the checkout counter, Saul sprang for a tote bag too.

"Woody Allen would like Saul Bellow to appear in a small part in his upcoming movie." Helen Robin from

*Emblematic flowers from Humboldt's Gift to The Dean's December, respectively.

Robert Greenhut Productions was on the phone.

I said, "What is it about?"

"Well, only Woody and Mia get to read the script. Woody does not give out the script or the story."

I said, "Yeah, but how's Saul going to know it's not about that jerk Saul Bellow?"

"No, it's nothing like that," she assured me. "It's going to be filmed on a Monday," and she gave me the date and said he would be given four pages of dialogue over the weekend, though he didn't have to do it word for word.

I said, " How much?" We haggled and finally stopped at five thousand dollars; it was going to be very short. Saul was to come into town on Sunday. On Saturday, I got a phone call from him.

"What have you got me doing? I don't even know what this is about. I don't know what my part is. How can I do this? I have no idea what it's all about."

I said, "They're going to send you a Federal Express packet at the hotel. Four pages. Only Woody and Mia know what the whole script is about."

"What is this? I can't do it. I have to know what this movie is about!"

The producer had given me his number in case anything happened over the weekend. I called, and he said, "What? Just tell him not to worry. He'll see the script, he'll see that it's okay. It's a story about a man who changes his character all the time, and Saul plays a man who's being interviewed who knew this man, and it's done in a documentary form. Are you telling me he's not going to do it?"

"Well, that's what he says."

So I called Saul and told him about it. "I don't know, I don't know," he said.

Saul came to town. Apparently, the producer called him several times at the hotel and told him everything was fine. The next morning, Saul came into my office, where he was supposed to be picked up at eleven. He put his head down, looking for a pill; his nose was running. He reached into his breast pocket. "I looked at the four paragraphs. I have four scenes. I'm not going to memorize it. I'm just getting the essence of it. I'll say what I have to say in my own words."

The doorbell rang. A burly man in a plaid jacket and a fedora hat and glasses came in. "You got a Bellow here?"

Saul went to the hall closet to get his coat.

"You Bellow? A station wagon's out front."

They went out. Saul looked scared, I had seen that same expression at the Nobel.

He came back about 2 P.M., all smiles.

"You know the driver who came to pick me up? Turns out he used to be a detective! Woody was very warm, he gave me a hug. And we went into the library, and I sat in a chair. No makeup or anything. Woody asked me the question and I gave him the answer. He said three of them were okay, but on the fourth one, he said, 'I don't mean the emphasis to be that way.' And did a retake."

At the invitation of the producers, I went to the screening of the movie. I invited Adam and his fiancée, Rachel, to come along. Saul was absolutely great. He didn't appear nervous. You could really believe he knew Zelig.

In addition to being a star of the silver screen, Saul's a recording artist. Caedmon Records was one of the first "spoken word" recording companies on which an author read from his/her work. I negotiated a contract for Saul to read from *Herzog*. He selected two scenes: on Side One, Sono, the Japanese girlfriend, on Side Two, Ramona, the European girlfriend.

It was a freezing, freezing day in Manhattan. The recording studio was in the garment district. We walked across town in the Thirties. There were all these men pushing clothes racks on snow-packed, icy sidewalks. We finally got inside. Saul was taken directly to the sound room to record. He was nervous. I could see he was nervous, because his nose was running. He always has to wipe his nose with a handkerchief or keep one close so that it doesn't run.

There were a few interruptions on Side One.

After a break, the director again explained, "Look, I'll interrupt you if we need to do a retake. You may have to do a number of retakes." Saul started reading side two, "Ramona." He was reading with such feeling! His face turned pink with pleasure. He read straight through—no retakes. I'd never heard such a great reading. Richard Burton couldn't have done it better.

We left. We went to the Bienvenue restaurant at Thirty-sixth and Madison. Saul's hands were freezing cold. They're usually warm.

"I have to tell you something. I made an appointment to see Rosette Lamont. [Ramona!] Her mother, Ludmilla, will be there. On Central Park West at two o'clock. I told Alexandra I was going to a museum."

It was very amusing to realize that in rehearsing the Ramona section for the recording, Saul got all caught up in Ramona again and made a date to see her.

"How will you go up there?"

"Subway. Her mother is going to be there. It's all right."

He came back to my office at four-thirty, relieved like someone who'd just been to a tax audit. After many, many years, he saw her, he saw her mother, they had a nice little visit. Then he left my office to go off and meet Alexandra.

Saul was invited by the International Poetry Forum to give a reading at Carnegie-Mellon in Pittsburgh. These dates are booked a year or nine months ahead. I called Saul.

Alexandra has a childhood friend, a biophysicist named Sanda Loga, who had also fled from Romania. Sanda escaped by marrying a German baron, who smuggled her out in a big doll box. He turned out to be a raving lunatic, and she ran away from him, got divorced, and moved to the United States, where she got a job in a laboratory at Carnegie-Mellon.

Saul called out, "Alexandra, do we want to go to Carnegie-Mellon in February? We can visit Sanda."

"That would be great."

I called back Samuel Hazo, made the arrangements, and told him about Sanda.

By the time February came around, Sanda had moved from Pittsburgh to Chicago. The weather was pretty bad, and Alexandra didn't want to go to Pittsburgh. Saul said, "What am I doing in Pittsburgh now?" So I offered to keep him company.

We met at Carnegie-Mellon and went to the auditorium. Saul read "A Silver Dish." The next day's *Pittsburgh Gazette* gave the reading a rave review, comparing it to a virtuoso violin recital. Saul used to play the "fiddle," as he calls it, and at one time considered becoming a professional violinist. He was especially thrilled.

Mark Harris, author of *Bang the Drum Slowly*, was also there. Mark and Saul go way back. For a number of years, he had been following Saul around to write his authorized biography (until authorization was taken away). Saul said hello and introduced me to Mark. They were cool.

The University of Georgia Press published a book called *Saul Bellow, Drumlin Woodchuck*, by Mark Harris. It was reviewed in *The New York Times*, and I ran out and bought a copy. I turned first to the last chapter, which was of Saul Bellow at Carnegie-Mellon. Harris had seen a notice that Saul was scheduled to read, so he went. From conversing earlier with director Hazo, Harris reckoned that there was really some woman that Saul was coming to see, some ophthalmologist, and that was the reason he accepted the reading. Arrangements had been made through Saul's secretary. (That was me.) He looked in the Pittsburgh Yellow Pages, trying to find women ophthalmologists. He couldn't find one. He went backstage and looked in the crowd, but he couldn't tell. There was some woman with him. (That was me.) She might have been the ophthalmologist.

Shows how rumors get started.

Pittsburgh again. A convocation of Nobel laureates was called to open the new convention center there.

Arrangements were made for Saul to give the inaugural address to a huge assemblage, including the governor, the mayor, and a hundred laureates.

The morning before the event, Saul took off from Chicago. I got a call about two o'clock. "I'm at the Detroit airport. There's a blizzard in Pittsburgh! The airport's officially closed there. I'm going to Cincinnati to stay with my niece Lesha overnight."

"You're giving the inaugural address! All those people are waiting for you. You're going to have the same trouble in Cincinnati!"

"Oh, no. I'm going to Cincinnati. The hell with that thing."

"Wait here. Let me at least call Pittsburgh first."

Okay.

"No, no! Don't let him go. We have twenty thousand people here and a hundred laureates. Keep him there!"

Saul calls me back. "I'm at American Airlines now."

"Stand by. A room at the airport hotel is being booked for you right now."

"I'm not going to the airport hotel. What am I doing in Detroit? I don't want to be in Detroit."

"Look, at least you can stay overnight. It doesn't do any good to go to Cincinnati. Stay where you are. Wait for me to page you. I'm going to see if Pittsburgh can get the hotel to send an escort to take your bags and check you in."

I have a lot of trouble connecting with Pittsburgh. We finally connect. The bellhop is confirmed.

I call the airline to page Saul Bellow. They page and page. No Saul Bellow.

About fifteen minutes later, Saul calls. "Did you try to get me? I stopped into the bar to have a drink, and you can't hear the page in there."

I tell him he's got a room and an escort is on the way.

Half an hour later, I get a call. This time it's from the hotel manager. A bellhop is at the airline, and Saul Bellow's not there.

It's about six o'clock. There's nothing for me to do but sit tight.

Twenty minutes later: "Hello, Harriet? I'm in my room in the hotel."

"But there's a bellhop waiting for you at American Airlines."

"Oh, I couldn't wait for him. I'm hungry. I'm going to get something to eat."

I said I'd stick around. Looking out the window, I watched the driving rain, trying to take it all in. He called me at seven and said he felt better.

"I just had a bite to eat at the restaurant at the airport."

"What did you have?"

"Duck à l'orange."

"You had duck à l'orange at an airport restaurant!"

He said it tasted like it was made with marmalade.

"Well, it probably was!"

Then he said, "You wouldn't want to come up, would you?"

I looked out the window and thought, No way! "I just can't. You'll be all right."

About 8 P.M., I got a phone call from Pittsburgh: We're going to send a Learjet because the airport is officially closed. I transmitted the message.

The next morning, I phoned one of the hosts to find out how Saul's doing. "He's fine. He's sleeping."

Five o'clock that evening, Saul calls from the Pittsburgh airport.

"Hi, Harriet!"

"How was it?"

"Great! This pilot came and knocked on my door at three o'clock in the morning and I was all alone with him on a jet and we had frozen doughnuts and cold coffee! We had a police escort because of the blizzard."

I must confess I told this story to Bernard and Ann Malamud at dinner the day after. Bernard looked up and said, "Harriet is Saul's mother and my grandmother."

*V.*

# Hometown Boy

*M*ayor Guy Descary of Lachine, Montreal, Quebec, had recently read flap copy of *The Dean's December* and discovered that Saul, winner of the Nobel Prize in literature, was a native son. The mayor called to tell me his plans: June 10, 1984, was to be proclaimed Saul Bellow Day. In the laureate's honor, the hometown public library would be officially renamed Bibliothèque Municipal Saul Bellow / Saul Bellow Public Library, with ceremony and much celebration. I told him that on that very day, Saul would be celebrating his sixty-ninth birthday.

I called Tom Victor, who often freelanced as a Time-Life photographer, and gave him the tip. Within fifteen minutes, he confirmed that *People* would cover the event. I reported this to Saul, who asked, "What do you think?"

"It sounds like a good idea, especially since *Him with His Foot in His Mouth and Other Stories* will be published this month."

"Okay. As long as they don't interfere."

Saturday morning, Tom and I met Josh Hammer, the writer *People* assigned, at JFK, and we all took Air Canada to Montreal. Sitting next to Tom, I cautioned him: Look, everything will be fine, but don't push with the photographing. Saul gives signals before he's unhappy. An unmistakable expression crosses his face. As soon as you see it, *stop*. It will pay off later. Otherwise you'll get nothing. Tom said okay.

We got to the Ritz-Carlton. The temperature outside was about 107 degrees, and it felt great to get inside. Saul happened to be in the lobby. I greeted him, and the boys went upstairs to their rooms.

Saul was very excited to be there, with his sister and niece and all the relatives gathered in Quebec.

"Remember my cousin Marvin and his wife, who take in Fresh Air Fund kids every summer at their ski lodge in

Vermont? They walked into the big family dinner last night, holding hands with a kid about ten years old, black, dressed in a prep school blazer and wearing goggles [Saul's word for eyeglasses]. Marvin introduces me to his adopted son, Lamont."

"Oh, you have a new cousin!" We both thought it was just great.

"How about that!"

"Cousins," one of my all-time favorite short stories, was in the new collection. It was about every kind of connection, from blood relative to member of the world family of man. (Remember the old grade school textbooks: My French Cousin, My Japanese Cousin . . .?)

A family luncheon was given by Mayor Descary for Saul on the hotel terrace.

Josh Hammer from People came into my room and asked if he could use the phone to call his father, also a writer, who held Saul Bellow in great esteem and had instructed his son to ring him on first sighting. "Dad, I'm here! I saw him! I met him! I'm going to talk with him!" I told Josh to relax. He left to prepare for the postprandial interview.

Mayor Descary generously invited me to a photo session on the terrace after lunch. The mayor himself took pictures. Alexandra had been upstairs all the while, correcting student papers. Oh, dear.

Midafternoon, Saul and Jane and I met Tom in the lobby.

Jane is nine years older than Saul and looks just like him but with red hair. I introduced Tom Victor to her.

"Oh! She's gorgeous. She's gorrrgeous." He turned to Jane. "You're just gorrrgeous."

Saul had a when's-this-going-to-end look on his face.

Jane looked as if this was the best thing that ever happened to her.

Tom had yet to snap the shutter. "Oh! I'd love to take a picture of you with Jane. She's gorrrgeous."

There was a piano in the lobby, and I spoke up with, "And Jane plays the piano."

Saul looked at me as if he'd bitten into an especially sour lemon.

We were driven to the old part of Montreal and let out to wander down those really hot streets. I'd had no idea we'd be walking and was wearing high heels that were already killing me.

Jane was shoulder-to-shoulder with her brother, and Tom was clicking away. You could see that Jane was really enjoying the moment. Tom was still not letting it drop. "Oh, you're gorrgeous."

Tom posed Saul, seated atop a fire hydrant, legs crossed at the ankles, Jane still in the frame.

Saul whispered to me, "My sister is in every one of these pictures."

"Ooh, look." Tom pointed. An ice cream store. "Ooh. Let's have a picture of Saul and Jane having ice cream cones!"

"Never mind, never mind," Saul snapped. By this time Saul had that expression on his face that says: Sixty seconds, and I lose it.

It was so hot. I was hobbling on my heels. I said to Tom, "Stop, stop. Enough!"

Just as I said this, Tom pointed and said, "Ooh, a horse and carriage. Let's have Saul and Jane in a horse and carriage."

Saul pulled me aside. "This is all your fault! You, Dr. Moriarty! You!! Are you trying to kill me?"

Now barely able to even hobble, I staggered over to Tom. The heat was dreadful, and I was in slow motion. He was already reiterating, "Oh Saul, how about you and Jane riding on the horse and carriage?"

Saul didn't say anything. He rushed to the limo waiting nearby, opened the door himself, got in, and slammed it shut. The car took off, leaving me, Jane, and Tom at the horse and carriage.

We took a cab back to the hotel, and in the lobby I scolded Tom "Don't *ever* do anything like that again! I told you."

"I have to get pictures!"

Back in my room, I collapsed on the bed and took my shoes off, in that order. No way am I ever going to get them back on. The phone rang. I picked it up. It's Saul. He's screaming. "Are you trying to kill me? I'm really angry. Really, really angry!"

I believed him. I don't think I ever heard anyone that angry. I thought he was going to burst a blood vessel.

"I just came from the elevator, and Tom tried to take my picture again. He asked me to put my tie back on! Are you trying to kill me?"

"I told him not to," I managed, barely audible.

An hour later, at about five o'clock, Josh rang in a panic. (I'd forgotten about him.) His tape recorder had malfunctioned, and there were a lot of blanks in the interview. Would I come right over and fill in some answers for him.

Okay. I go.

Tom wanders in from his adjoining suite; I let him have it. Josh leaves the room, Tom blows up at me. Josh returns, and we all go out for dinner. Tom and I are not speaking but shooting daggers at each other, Josh worries nonstop about the interview.

Early next morning, Tom rang, all bright and cheery. "We're all downstairs, waiting for you, Saul and Alexandra and the mayor. We're off to visit the house where Saul was born."

A few minutes later, Saul was on the phone, all bright and cheery. "Tom says you're not coming. Is that true?"

"You've already got a full limo." I was still smarting.

The car ride to Lachine takes half an hour. Spanky new bilingual signs on the highway point the way to "Saul Bellow Public Library," out on the front lawn of which the covered plaque is waiting to be unveiled. The full band, in regalia, banners flying. The whole town has gathered.

Noonish, the limousine pulled up. Saul, Jane, Alexandra, niece Lesha, Tom, and M. Descary emerged. Alexandra greeted me. "We missed you."

"I was hiding out."

"I thought so."

Saul, immediately surrounded by autograph seekers, not to mention writers eager to hand him copies of their novels, threw me a sidelong glance. "Oh, here's my agent. You can talk to her about your manuscript."

The mayor, standing by Saul's side, made the formal dedication, and the plaque was revealed. M. Descary made the surprise announcement that this day also marked the *anniversaire de naissance* of Lachine's man of the hour. The band struck up, and the whole crowd sang

"Happy Birthday." Saul, surprised and pleased at this added attraction, stood at the podium. He began a brilliant and moving bilingual address from the heart, on the meaning of one's birthplace, one's origins. In French he related one of his earliest recollections: being told by his mother that she found him in a bucket floating on the ocean, her version of the stork, which he had truly believed.

Next, everyone into the library to view the special exhibit, then on to a grand luncheon, and finally to the city hall for closing toasts in the mayor's office with his staff.

*People* magazine ran the article the following week, with many photos by Thomas Victor. Not one of Jane.

A few days later, back home, in talking about the event and Mayor Descary, Saul remarked, "He's smart. He's politically ambitious. Probably has his eye on prime minister."

P.S. Some references erroneously list Saul Bellow's birth date as July 10, 1915. In the early twenties, the Lachine town hall burned down, and affidavits were required to replace lost records. A Bellow family representative listed the month of July, Saul's mother, Lisa, assured him he was born on June 10, and "she ought to know." The destruction of the old records provided an opportunity to change Saul's first name after his life-threatening bout with peritonitis, before antibiotics, at the age of seven, confined to a ward for terminally ill children. As I understand it, it used to be customary to change the name of a gravely ill Jewish child so as to deceive death.

This near fatal childhood experience had a profound influence on his beginnings as a writer: waking up to find missing roommates and empty hospital beds almost daily, being allowed visits from one parent at a time, every other week, having only the New Testament and the funny papers to read, being blessed with a rich imagination, and given much time for thinking and trying to make sense of the world.

As for the surname, all of Saul's relatives use "Bellows." Saul chose to transliterate the Cyrillic spelling on his mother's passport, "ßΕλογ," dropping the "s" for himself and his progeny.

Later in the year, Saul and Alexandra came to town. He was to read for The Writer's Voice at the West Side Y. There was such an overflow that the auditorium of the Society for Ethical Culture, at Sixty-third Street and Central Park West, had to be used.

They checked into the Mayflower Hotel, two blocks away, earlier that day. I met Saul in the lobby, and went up to their room. It was before the hotel was renovated. There was such an accumulation of new paint over old on the windows and doors that you could barely open or shut them. Saul was still sort of casing the room. We both looked down. From outside the bathroom, approaching the bed, there were little brown spots on the carpet. Neither of us said a word.

He began to unpack, he reached into his jacket pocket. "Look at this." In his hand was a tiny silver purse with a silver chain. It had been his mother's, and before she died she had given it to him and told him to take care of it. It had become his good-luck charm. Whenever he lectured or read in public, he told me, he kept it in his pocket.

He finished unpacking, went to the bathroom, came out. "What? You think that's ca-ca on the floor?" he said, as we left the room.

His reading that night was a huge success. As the audience filed out to the reception, I heard a satisfied listener describe it very well: "This tired old man shuffled on stage. As he read, he turned young and bouncy again."

I shuffled home at about eleven. Exhausted. The phone rings. It's Saul. Hysterical.

"My mother's purse! I left my mother's purse on the lectern! I have to have it!"

"Take it easy. I'll call Jason." He was the director, and

I remembered he was going off to a trendy Japanese nightclub in SoHo.

I managed to get him on the phone, barely audible through the Friday-night din.

"We have a huge crisis. Saul forgot his mother's silver purse, his lucky piece, on the lectern. He promised his mother he would take care of it, and he's really, really upset. Can you send someone over there?"

"I don't have the key to the Ethical Culture Building. But listen, it's completely locked now, and I remember looking around after everyone went down to the reception. Tell him not to worry. No one's been back in that room. We'll get it tomorrow morning, first thing, when it opens at seven-thirty."

I called Saul back. "Not to worry. The purse will be in your hands at seven-thirty in the morning."

"I have to have it! I promised my mother I would take care of it. Can't he call the police? If it were Mayor Koch and his mother's purse, they'd open it up for him. I can't wait till seven-thirty in the morning." He was beside himself.

"Saul, try to sleep easy. You took care of that purse all those years. If this is the destiny of the purse, then this is the destiny of the purse. It was meant to be." I kept repeating that, trying to calm him down. He kept repeating,

"My mother told me to take care of it, and now it's lost!"

The next morning, Jason telephones me. "I went to the Ethical Culture School. They opened it up. I have the purse."

"Call him!"

"I did! I'm in the Mayflower Hotel coffee shop now. He's supposed to come down and meet me."

When we met later that morning, Saul was walking on air.

After renting for some years in Vermont, Saul and Alexandra wanted to own a house on land of their own. I was surprised Saul wanted to build, not buy an old farmhouse. He bought some property, designed the house himself, and engaged his neighbor and all-around jack-of-all-trades, craftsman Frank Maltese, to build it, a lifetime dream for each.

A carpenter, a contractor, and an electrician, Frank had never built an entire house on his own. Saul was very proud of designing it and called me with progress reports throughout its construction.

I never saw a house so well made in my life. There wasn't a crooked anything. Everything fit. You could tell it was built with absolute love and great care. There weren't any cracks. There weren't any spaces. It was perfect, seamless.

You could see Frank Maltese's pleasure and pride every time he passed by or stopped in.

From the front porch, you walked into a huge kitchen with a slate floor, which looked like a synthesis of all the kitchens Saul had ever read about in novels, and there was the biggest fireplace I'd ever seen outside of a castle. In the TV room, between the kitchen/dining room and the living room, there was a flowered sofa—big flowers—with skirts and ruffles all around. It looked exactly like a huge, frumpy dumpling of a woman. I had never seen a couch like that in my life. Oversized, wide, deep, with the plumpest cushions. I laughed every time I looked at it. It certainly had personality: another character in a living Bellow novel.

In the next room, Saul had his typewriter, the music stand where he rested his ledger book, and a violin.

The bathroom has a skylight roof. Saul likes to look at the stars in the middle of the night. (An experience not to be missed, I can tell you.)

A year later, Saul built a huge, screened-in studio, Japanese style, way back in the woods. With a futon inside, a table for his typewriter, and a little deck with a couple of chairs, it was a sanctuary, unviolated. Until ...

The Saul Bellow Society was started by a number of professors from various colleges and universities around the country. The society puts out a newsletter and the *Saul Bellow Journal* (SBJ), published twice a year. Saul refuses to acknowledge the existence of the organization and the publication. He says it feels like a monument to the dead. He doesn't think there should be such a thing for a writer during his lifetime.

An international conference on the work of Saul Bellow was held in April 1987 in Haifa. There were many speakers, including Martin Amis. Attending was the entire Saul Bellow Society, which organized a package trip for its members. One of the participants reported to me. There were two contingents—Saul Bellow and the Saul Bellow Society. Saul Bellow avoided the Society the whole time. One officer of the Society and of SBJ apparently was so fired up by the events and determined to meet with the Master that when she returned to the States, she decided to do some private-eye work to discover Saul Bellow's well-hidden whereabouts in Vermont.

One day, Saul was sitting writing in his private screened-in studio in the woods. He looked up and found himself face-to-face with the Saul Bellow Society and Journal, who expressed great pride in having found him and was excitedly giving him the details of her investigation, which, he told me later, he interrupted by ordering her angrily off the premises—and fast.

It's really amazing anyone did find him. Stanley must have had an easier time tracking down Livingston.

Saul was working on *More Die of Heartbreak* during the summer of 1985, the last time I visited him and Alexandra in Vermont. When I arrived, the atmosphere was extremely tense. Saul had been telling me that Alexandra was going into rages. She couldn't get the safety cap off the medicine bottle, and took a knife and sort of sawed it off. He thought it was scary. I kept quiet, but I've done that more than once myself with a screwdriver or can opener. Who thought up those bottle caps anyway?

I got there late that evening with two pounds of corned beef. When Saul opened the bag, he got all depressed. It turned out that his cousin's deli in Chicago had just been closed temporarily by the Department of Health because some of his corned beef had given some of his customers salmonella poisoning. So there I was with two pounds of beautiful lean corned beef, and he freaked. He barely ate it. The slice he had, for my sake, he heated up red-hot.

Alexandra was very polite, but they barely spoke to each other. For several years, they used to take me to visit a friend, Mary Gray Hughes and her husband, who lived about an hour away. Mary Gray happened to be a friend of Tillie Olsen. She adored Tillie, thought she was the greatest. After Diarmuid Russell died, I had worked with Tillie at R&V on her novel fragment *Yonnandio*, her nonfiction *Silences*, and the motion picture rights to *Tell Me a Riddle*, with Melvyn Douglas (his last film) and Lila Kedrova, directed by Lee Grant.

Next day, we were sitting around the table after lunch, and Alexandra said to me hesitantly, "Mary Gray Hughes would love you to come and visit."

Saul said, "You don't have to go if you don't want to."

I was getting stuck in the middle.

She said, "If you don't want to come it's okay, but I told her you would be coming. They really like you."

And Saul said, "You don't have to go if you don't want to."

I had to let Alexandra save face: it was her friend who had invited me. I said, "I'll go." She was so happy, a big smile came on her face.

I may have incurred Saul's wrath, but it was worth it to see that smile of hers. And when Alexandra left the room, I said to Saul, "I must do this."

"Okay, you do what you want." (It seemed, actually, to be Saul's respect that I had incurred.)

She and I drove out. We had a nice visit. The Hugheses didn't quite understand why Saul wasn't there. Every time I'd come to Vermont in the last few years, all of us went to see them.

"Where's Saul?" Mary Gray's husband asked.

"Oh, he had some work to do. He sends his regards."

Bob Hughes started telling a story, "which Saul would really love." During the Spanish Inquisition, I think it was, "they used to behead impotent men."

Hardly a subject for a couple whose marriage is on the rocks.

You should have seen Alexandra. I was thinking: Good thing he isn't here.

At first Saul loved that Alexandra—a mathematician— was not a verbal person, her English somewhat halting. Nowhere near the Master! Lately he had taken to teasing her with jokes and statements she couldn't quite follow.

That night, we had a pretty tense drink before going out to dinner at their favorite place, Le Petit Chef. Stalin's daughter had returned to the Soviet Union, and Saul asked Alexandra, "Why do you suppose Svetlana left the West?"

"I don't know."

"Do you think it has to do with men? There aren't any strong men in the West?"

"I don't know."

"Do you think that it could be?"

"I suppose it could."

"How do you like that? My wife says there are no strong men in the West. This is how she talks about her husband?"

"Come on, Saul. Cut it out," I said.

Alexandra looked completely bewildered, as if mystified that what started out as cocktail chat in a relaxed mood had spun around and taken such a swift dive.

We rode to the restaurant in silence, but during the meal, Alexandra, and Saul too, softened a little. I told Alexandra a joke that she really got a kick out of, and it changed the tone of the evening: A guy goes into a bar and sits down. He has a frog on his head. The bartender doesn't say anything, gets his order, pours him a drink and then another. Finally, the bartender can't resist. He says, "What's this all about?" "I don't know. He just grew out of my ass one day," the frog answers.

Alexandra let out a hearty laugh. It hit her as a real thigh-slapper.

Earlier, she had gone to the video store and picked up *Godfather* II and *Key Largo* to watch after dinner. On the way back, things were mellower. Saul and I were singing "Stardust"—I, the Willie Nelson rendition. Alexandra would burst out in a laugh every once in a while, remembering the frog. When we got to the house, Alexandra said, "I'm going upstairs for a sweater." As soon as she ascended the steps to the bedroom, Saul ran to the kitchen table, grabbed the bag with the tapes, practically skidded to a halt at the VCR, and stuck in a cassette. I said, "Saul, Alexandra is coming down, and she'll miss the first part of *Godfather II*" (which was important, as neither of them had seen *Godfather I*). "That's all right. That's all right." He sat back in his seat, all excited with the satisfaction of one-upmanship. She came down after ten minutes and seemed startled that we had begun without her. Saul sat in front of the VCR, looking as if he were totally wrapped up in the film.

It had been a season of death for Saul. He was now seventy. When he was sixty, he'd said he hated being sixty. Each year he'd say, "I hate being sixty-one . . . sixty-two . . . " And I'd say, "You're not getting old—you're not old. The only reason you're sixty-nine is that last year you were sixty-eight and the year before that you were sixty-seven . . . " The week after his seventieth (three score and ten) birthday, he made a trip to New York. We were walking on Thirty-sixth Street, toward my office, and I noticed he was shuffling, slightly stooped, his breathing labored. "I'm seventy years old now," he said.

"Yes, but just a week ago you were only sixty-nine years old. Straighten up, walk briskly."

"It's not a rational thing, intellectually I understand that."

A few weeks later, not a month after his seventieth birthday, both of his older brothers died. He had rushed down to Florida to reunite with the estranged Morris, but he got there too late. There was to be no closure. As soon as this brother passed on, Saul began to tell all sorts of anecdotes and to talk about him in glowing terms. Then his dear brother Sam died of the same disease, prostate cancer.

Right on the heels of his brothers' deaths, Saul's marriage died.

When he and Alexandra went back to Chicago in the fall, Saul called me and said, "We decided we needed to fix up the whole apartment. New drapery, new couch, new rugs." I guess that was their way of trying to make it work again. They did get all those things, then he called me and said, "It's impossible."

After one argument, Alexandra threw photos of Saul into the garbage. A knock on the door a few days later. It was the porter, holding an eight-by-ten glossy he found in the trash bin. He asked Saul to inscribe it to him.

Shortly thereafter, Saul and Alexandra separated.

On the night of March 18, 1986, unable to sleep, I turned the radio on. Suddenly I heard, "The Pulitzer Prize–winning author Bernard Malamud was found dead in his apartment." I jumped out of bed. I've been afraid to listen to the radio like that ever again.

Shortly after Bernard died, Saul went to London to address the PEN International Congress. Seeing how glum he was, I said: "Would you like me to visit you after you come back from London?"

Philip Roth and Claire Bloom were living in London. And Saul, unhappy in his hotel, some place near Harrod's that everybody else liked, called Philip and asked if he could get him a room at his club. Philip did. They were riding in a London taxi together, and Saul, staring out the window, said, "Now only Hart and Schaffner are left." (Hart, Schaffner & Marx was a popular men's clothing manufacturer in the fifties and sixties. Bellow, Roth, and Malamud were always linked together by the press.)

It was Easter weekend when Saul got back. I flew to Chicago.

Saul had moved into a new flat in Hyde Park. A university van dropped me off a block and a half away, and I passed Allan Bloom's apartment house, the Cloisters, where Saul had lived when I first visited him, way back when. The next building was Saul's. I'm waiting in the lobby for the elevator, and who walks in, carrying a percolator, but Janis Freedman, his twenty-eight-year-old student-secretary, who'd helped him move and, at Alexandra's urging, helped "comfort him." We communicated quite frequently about business, but I hadn't told her I was coming. I was sort of embarrassed, and she was startled to see me there with my suitcase. Saul's percolator had broken, she told me, and he'd asked her to get a new one. I didn't believe it was coincidence that we ran into each other. But at the time, I just thought: how odd. I think that when I phoned him from the airport, he called her and said, Could you get me a percolator, and could you get it now?

The apartment was beautiful, his favorite color green couch and all. The books were set up on the shelves, bookshelves on practically every wall, and Janis had helped him. I noticed potential peril immediately, having developed a trained eye from some well-intentioned office assistants over the years. The books were aligned with the front edge instead of against the back of the shelf, so all the weight's in the front; the books threaten to fall forward en masse. Quickly and quietly, I went around pushing them to the back.

That day in Chicago we went shopping. Saul enjoys

shopping; it's a big thing; he seems to find it very rewarding. First, we looked for a straw wastebasket for his new studio, then on to the fish store and to the supermarket for pineapple. Saul likes cooking, feels a real sense of achievement in cooking something well. We ran into a professor he knew who looked like Bela Lugosi, black hat and all. He had a Lucite cane and was a real philosopher.

Saul showed me more of his place. In a walk-in closet was a wooden file cabinet. It was a file cabinet with a history. Not long after Stockholm, I came to Chicago to help Saul find file cabinets made of wood so they would look good in his new apartment. The wall of the apartment next door to Alexandra's had been broken through to provide bigger quarters. It was a very snowy day. And in Chicago, it really snows. Piles and piles of snow all over the place, which terrifies me. I'll fall and break a leg or an arm or a head. I hate it. We slipped and slid to any number of office furniture showrooms downtown. No wooden files, only fireproof steel, with locks.

I went back to New York, and there in the *Times* was an ad for "Wooden File Cabinets by Unbelievable Aronson." I ordered a two-drawer horizontal for Saul and, while I was at it, a vertical for my office.

If he was going to keep it in the closet, he might as well have had a steel cabinet.

I went to my room and changed as he made dinner. Fish marsala, his own salad with start-from-scratch dressing. In the dining room, I noticed he now had family pictures up: his parents, himself when he was little, the old-country thing.

I had brought him a movie video of *Lovesick*, in which Dudley Moore plays a psychiatrist whose first name is Saul. A young, very attractive patient comes in and lies on the couch, and he absolutely falls in love with her. She tells him she had a dream that she was at a party, and this man named Herzog came over to her.

He asks: "Why the name Herzog?"

"Gee, I don't know."

That's the name of a novel. Do you know who wrote it?"

"No."

"Bellow."

"Oh," she says, "Saul Bellow."

("That's me!" Saul uttered, momentarily disoriented.)

I had brought Saul a Chinese box for his paper clips and a bottle of Poire William brandy, with a whole pear grown inside.

We sat down to eat. He looked at me and said, "You know, for over twenty years we've spoken to each other at least once a day. I'm so glad you're here."

He said, "Finish your fish. You didn't finish your fish. You never finish your meals"—a reference, I inferred, to that night he first came to my house for dinner and brought the 135 pages of Humboldt's Gift.

Sometimes, since then, I'd wondered: Does he remember?

He certainly did.

The next night, Allan Bloom prepared dinner at his place. I was to look at his blue-penciled manuscript, still called "American Nihilism." Bloom made a joint—as they say in England. The roast slipped off the plate: typical Bloom. In the corner near the entrance to the dining room was a particularly gangly, lackluster palm tree. Bloom was running back and forth, back and forth, back and forth, in and out of the kitchen. Saul and I watched as the fronds brushed the seat of his pants every time he passed. Finally, Saul, who thought that plant was the ugliest plant he'd ever seen, burst out, "Allan, now I know what that plant's good for."

I had been reading while we had drinks. I had been reading while Bloom prepared dinner.

He came out of the kitchen, saying, "You know, they're

not having any advertising for this, and they're only planning to print ten thousand copies."

I said, "Well, the book's a miracle in itself."

He kept saying, "Don't you think it's going to be a best-seller? Don't you think it's going to sell at least fifty thousand copies?"

When he got back into the kitchen, Saul said, "Don't you think it's going to be a best-seller?"

I said, "Are you kidding? Only by a fluke."

Allan came back. I said, "Now look, I know you envision your book in pyramids in bookstore windows across the country. It's possible, but you can't count on it."

"But you certainly think it will sell at least forty thousand copies."

I said, "You got to say what you wanted to say, it's going to be published. We'll see what happens."

Two months later, Saul asked me to come to Vermont—a kind of 911 call. It was Memorial Day weekend, and instead of flying directly from New York to New Orleans to attend the American Booksellers Association annual convention, I made a twenty-four-hour stopover in New England.

Saul was standing at the kitchen sink, downcast. "I'm all alone," he said.

"Well, you've been married four times and are alone.

I've never been married and I'm alone."

He looked up at me. "The difference is I have three sons."

That June, Adam invited me to his outdoor wedding in Riverdale. Adam and Rachel Newton stood together between two majestic trees, young, full of hope, exchanging vows in front of the rabbi who performed the ceremony. Saul stood against the tree at the right, all in white—white suit and panama hat—facing Adam's mother, Sandra, in a big picture hat, who stood against the tree on the left. I was suddenly aware of watching what could have been a scene from Delmore Schwartz's "In Dreams Begin Responsibilities." It was heart-stopping: The two parents framing the young couple, and glaring at each other. I imagined them as a young couple all those years earlier, taking the same vows.

Saul was seventeen when his mother died of breast cancer, three years after a mastectomy. He was the youngest child in the family by almost ten years, and his sister and brothers, as well as his father, were at work during the day throughout mother's illness. As soon as school was out, Saul would come home and stay by her side in the kitchen, helping her. They became very close.

It was from her that he learned to cook and clean, passions of his to this day.

When Daniel was fourteen, one hot, dry, very sunny day in Vermont in July, Saul and I were sitting outside on Adirondack chairs. I was looking out over the countryside, and, city girl that I am, I said, "What a beautiful large lawn you have."

Very quietly, very understated, Saul corrected me: "It's a meadow."

Daniel came out and began to cut the grass on what was his father's lawn. Saul watched him. Suddenly he turned to me. "When I was Daniel's age, my mother was sitting with me outside on a day like this. She took her blouse off because she thought the sun would be healing." Saul saw the terrible scar of the missing breast, and she said to him, "You see. This is why your father doesn't come near me anymore."

It struck me, then, that Saul had really been traumatized at an early age. The seven-year-old boy in the ward for the terminally ill and the fourteen-year-old who had to stay by his mother's side are still there. At the Nobel banquet, Saul said: "the child in me is delighted, and despite appearances there is a child." Literally, very much alive.

In October, I entered the hospital to have what was to be a simple gallbladder operation. I dreaded hospitals and didn't go until I had no other choice. It was the first time I'd been out of my office since the beginning of my agency. Before I even arrived, Saul sent me a plant with a note: Love, Saul.

It was to be a four-day stay. Everything went wrong. I developed a staph infection on the table, which went unnoticed for a week, until my blood pressure dropped dramatically. I became comatose, my kidneys failed, and I was rushed off to intensive care, barely alive.

Miraculously, I got out of the ICU and into a room with a telephone. I was on dialysis, but there wasn't a day when I wasn't doing some work. The agency was running.

Way before I entered the hospital, I had completed negotiations for Saul's next novel, More Die of Heartbreak, to be published by Morrow. The contract with this new publisher had been officially signed but not yet announced. Saul had left Harper & Row after two books.

The day before I was discharged, Ed McDowell of The New York Times called. "Is it true that Saul is going to Morrow?"

"Yes."

I had shampoo all over my hair—the first time I'd washed it in seven weeks—and doctors and nurses were trooping in and out of my room.

"Did he do it for money?"

"No. He's not a money writer. He's a writer because it's his trade."

The next day, the item appeared in the "Book Notes" column of the *Times*. It made a big impression on everybody in the hospital, and on everyone else, it looked as if I had negotiated the contract while in the ICU and on the dialysis machine.

One day in March 1987, four months post-op, I had a phone bill totaling seven hours (420 minutes) to Chicago. That day, I had taken down Saul's corrections to proofs of *More Die of Heartbreak* in a yellow highlighter. It was the first thing I could grab, writing like crazy as he dictated. I didn't want to break his concentration by looking for another pen. Imagine, all day, by the window light. The proofs had to be at the publisher next morning. When I was finished, it was dark. I was waiting for Saul's favorite copy editor, Marge Horvitz, to come over to transcribe the changes onto the master set of proofs. I called down for something to eat, and when I looked at the proofs again, I realized I couldn't read a word I had put down with that highlighter—the page seemed to absorb the yellow like a blotter. It was absolutely illegible. I was exhausted and shaky and about to die of heartbreak/heart attack myself, so foggy and so upset I couldn't think clearly. I just kept trying to make out what I couldn't make out. Marge got there, and she was able to adjust the lamp in a slant that allowed her to read the yellow squiggles. Marge saved the day. After she transferred my notes, she got on the phone to Saul for close to another hour, with questions of her own. When she left, I cried in relief. I just sat there and cried.

As I returned to health and to my own new life in 1987, the ten-thousand-copy first printing of Allan Bloom's "American Nihilism," now entitled The Closing of the American Mind, was published.

Saul said to Allan, "Now you'll see what a lousy racket this is."

Bloom's book was a once-in-a-lifetime success.

The Thursday before Easter, my phone rings. "The Closing of the American Mind is number eleven on next week's New York Times best-seller list." It was too soon after publication to even think of the best-seller list! Ten thousand books had been printed, three thousand were in the warehouse, and seven thousand were in the stores. All the reviews came at once, so no matter where people looked—TV, radio, newspapers—within a two-week period they were somewhere made aware of the book. That's likely what made it catch fire. William Buckley called, MacNeil/Lehrer called. *Newsweek* did a spread, *Time* did a spread, the *Washington Post* did a spread in the Style section. It all happened at once.

I pass the Doubleday bookstore at Fifty-seventh and Fifth, and it's in the window!

I had said to Allan, Look, I know you envision your books in pyramids in bookstore windows across the country . . . but—and there it was! After that, it was one rapid thing after another. I called Bob Asahina, Allan's editor, and Bob said they were flying out of the stores. Then there was a cartoon in *The New Yorker* and one in the *Washington Post.* Allan Bloom called me and said, "Can't you talk to Snyder?" The following week, it jumped from eleven to five! I called Dick Snyder, publisher and CEO of Simon & Schuster, and he said, "I know! I know! Believe me, I'll look after this man!" Then Bloom got his friend Leonard Garment, who used to be Nixon's lawyer, to call his pal Dick Snyder and sort of reinforce. Dick said, "I'm going to go for a twenty-five-thousand-a-week reprint." So it went from number eleven to five, then to four.

On Wednesday afternoon, *The New York Times* has its *Book Review* meeting and closes its list for the Sunday after next. You can call a special number on Thursday morning and find out the best-sellers for the following week.

Obsessively, I began doing that. I gave Allan the number and I had him doing it. I thought I'd give it a try one Wednesday evening and caught it just as it was recorded. *The Closing of the American Mind* was number one! So he called the number, and he couldn't get anything. "Are you sure you're not making it up?" The whole night, we kept trying, each without the other knowing it. I kept getting a busy signal, and he kept getting a busy signal, the next morning, we decided our calls had been canceling each other out. Finally, he heard. And the first thing he said was, "I wonder how long I'm going to stay number one." For weeks it held there. Both hardcover and softcover were on the list for a year.

Dick Snyder began personally taking a hand in day-to-day sales. He and I became friendly doing business together. I asked when the first royalty statement was due and if he could tell me how much it was going to be. Some publishing companies keep up to forty percent of an author's royalties to protect themselves against unsold books that are sent back by bookstores later, could Simon & Schuster not hold the usual reserve against returns? Dick told me how much Allan's first royalty was going to be, and I said, "This book is going to do more, then there's the paperback, he really needs a nice round number. Couldn't you make it a little more?" And he made it a lot more. He gave Allan a very nice round number, and I sent Dick Snyder a dozen red roses. He said it was the first time anyone (let alone an agent!) had sent him a dozen red roses.

So I had this check to bring to Bloom. I called him and said I was coming to Chicago on a Friday, would stay overnight, and was going to bring him his first royalty check. It was a whopping amount of money! I asked him what his favorite restaurant was. I was going to stay at the Drake, and he was going to meet me there. I was going to send a car to pick him up. I had the car take us to this Japanese restaurant of his choice. I had put the check in a regular letter envelope. I put that in a 10 x 12 envelope, which I put in a $13^1/_2$ x $15^1/_2$ envelope. That I placed in one of those accordion folders with a string around it, which I dropped in a book mailer. I addressed each one of them to Allan Bloom.

We were having drinks, and his eyes were flashing. "Would you like to have your check now?" I handed him this huge book bag. He opened it up, then pulled out the legal-size accordion folder. Laughter. Then he opened the first mailer envelope, laughed. I could tell he was going crazy. His hands were trembling as he opened each envelope. Finally, he got to the check. He certainly did like the look of that check!

The next day, I went with him to buy some Persian rugs from his "special dealer." I think the merchants saw

him coming, as the saying goes. They ushered him past
the showroom—"Oh, no, no, no, these are not for *you*,
Mr. Bloom"—and they brought him down into the inner
sanctum, where there were rugs worthy of the
taste/pocketbook of Mr. Bloom. Just take the rugs to try.
He could pay later if he kept them. Of course, getting
them out of the store and into his apartment was the
biggest part of the sale. After Allan's death, Saul said,
"Allan sure was taken on those rugs. The IRS valued them
at much less than he paid."

Before we went shopping, Allan asked me up for a
post-breakfast coffee, while he waited for a delivery. He
loved coffee. He had a state-of-the-art industrial-size
copper cappuccino machine and coffeemaker—his pride
and joy. When he greeted me at the door, he was wearing
a full-length gray raw-silk kimono, tied with a wide sash
in the traditional fashion.

Allan was well over six feet tall and bald, with just the
merest fringe above his ears. To me, he looked and spoke
like Milton Berle before a nose job. Looking at Allan, I
couldn't help thinking of Uncle Miltie any more than I
could help thinking of the Lone Ranger every time I heard
the *William Tell* overture.

He loved to eat, he loved to drink, he loved to smoke. He
wasn't heavy, but looked well fed.

His ears were outstanding, but he was no Clark Gable, by any means. Speaking of his critics and detractors, Allan once told me, "It's my big funny ears people don't like, not my politics or prose."

In his apartment, he had imported the most beautiful huge glass-top coffee table, a gorgeous soft black leather couch, and a red overstuffed chair that clashed: almost an orange red, it didn't fit with the red reds in the room. There were beautiful art deco lamps and tables. Allan saw me looking at the red chair. "That chair doesn't fit, does it? Saul *insisted* that I buy it. I shouldn't have listened to him, but he insisted."

That morning, a salesman came from Marshall Field to install a Lalique chandelier in the dining room. He brought with him a huge Lalique bowl that had the very same leaf design as the chandelier. He said: "I'm just bringing this here, you might want to have this." And he brought six Lalique wineglasses. "And you might want to have these." Allan asked me what I thought, and I thought it was *de trop*. I got a dirty look from Marshall Field!

Saul said Allan's "attitude toward money was that it was something to be thrown away, scattered from the rear platform of trains." But the first thing he did was pay off all his debts. Then he bought and surrounded himself with beauty: medieval tapestry, Renaissance paintings, a 2,300-year-old Greek torso on a stand. A male, headless, armless, and legless. And you could rotate it too. He bought himself a pair of black speakers and lots of CDs. I'd never seen such speakers before: the height of doors, on either side of the living room. He turned up the volume full blast and conducted Viennese marches! You could feel it vibrating through all your bones.

By June, *More Die of Heartbreak* came on *The New York Times* best-seller list at fourteen. The prerecorded message announced, "*More Die of Heart Attack.*" I'd learned how to phone and get a preview of the list as it was being prepared for release, so I was able to get a correction spliced in before too many listeners heard the gaffe.

Allan's book was at one or two. Saul's novel was on the list for some weeks but hovered at the middle, nine or ten, except for a couple of weeks when it shot up to four, but then it dropped down and off the list. Allan would say, "And what's Saul . . . aw, he's number eleven? Aw, I feel bad for Saul!"

I used to call Allan the Number One Most Wanted Man in America. His opinion was sought everywhere. When he went off to Paris, I would send a cable every Thursday, telling him in French or in some kind of code his number on the best-seller list.

Coming to New York to do the *MacNeil/Lehrer Newshour*, he stayed at the Plaza Hotel. The Puerto Rican Day Parade was passing on Fifth Avenue, and he tried to persuade a little kid who was wearing a "Numero Uno" button to let him buy the button—the kid wouldn't sell at any price! Allan proceeded down Fifth Avenue and stopped in at a Doubleday bookstore. "You know, nobody recognized me! My picture is not on the cover." That's when I called photographer Jerry Bauer, who quickly brought his camera to the Plaza. Subsequent editions ran a photo on the flap. Allan appeared on almost all the shows—Evans and Novak, *Open Mind*, ABC, NBC, CBS, PBS, CNN—but he longed for only one: "I want Oprah. I want Oprah." Then one day, quite a number of months after his book came out, I had the great pleasure of calling him. "Oprah wants you!" He was thrilled out of his mind!

The theme of the program was General Knowledge, and it opened with a quiz of the audience. One of the questions: "What is the Magna Carta?" Oprah pointed the microphone at some guy, who answered "It's a bottle of champagne!" Then she asked, "Does the earth move around the sun, or does the sun move around the earth?" Oprah pointed her microphone, and this woman answered, "I think the sun moves around the earth, because we don't feel it!" Then a schoolteacher was asked, "Who was the second president of the United States?" She didn't know! There was one more question. It was a very good one: "What is Gdansk?" And somebody answered, "A polka."

Then Oprah brought out Allan Bloom. He loved being on her show. He said she was just wonderful. He loved her. She felt the material of his suit and complimented him.

It was the highlight of his life . . . and it was almost canceled. In Chicago, the program is seen live in the morning, then, it's syndicated on tape in the afternoon. The live taping was interrupted by a local news bulletin: Mike Ditka, the coach of the Chicago Bears, had had a heart attack. Allan nearly had a heart attack himself! Here's his chance to be on the Oprah Winfrey show, and it was going to be preempted! But the show went on.

By 1988, *The Closing of the American Mind* was a worldwide best-seller and had been on *The New York Times* list for over a year. Bloom became a millionaire and a celebrity, and the title was a windfall for the agency—the biggest commercial success for HWLA, Inc., at the time. I negotiated his next book with Simon & Schuster and became his lecture agent too.

Allan's ninety-year-old mother, whom he adored, had had a stroke. The doctors weren't sure of how much she was aware or unaware. Allan flew to Philadelphia to see her, walked into her hospital room. She said, "I know who you are. You wrote *The Closing of the American Mind*."

Allan Bloom had become another real-life character in a living Saul Bellow novel.

Saul, always very eager to enjoy Allan's company and conversation, was especially so in Vermont, where he invited him for a stay a couple of summers running. Before his second visit, Allan asked me if I knew a nice place in Martha's Vineyard where he could stay before going to Saul's place: "I need to be in shape to spend some time in the Green Mountains with Saul. I want to go and relax, and he wants to talk about Nietzsche, Rousseau, etc. I've got to be on my toes the whole time."

I consulted and was told the name of a quiet retreat, a good place to stay. The following year, when I went to Martha's Vineyard myself for the first time and stayed in Edgartown, the hub of the Vineyard, I went to find the place I had recommended to Allan, the number-one-best-selling author. It was deep in the woods, the way there approached by a dirt path until there was barely an opening wide enough for a car to get through. Almost completely inaccessible. I thought: Oh, poor Allan, stuck in the back of beyond. And I understood what he meant when, asked whether the place was satisfactory, he told me it was a little out of the way and he had to hire a car every day (he couldn't drive) to take him to Edgartown for any kind of social life and to the bookstore that carried copies of *The Closing of the American Mind*.

I felt terrible when I realized that the ideal place for him would have been the very hotel in town at which I was now staying.

Not too long after publication, Saul and I were heading toward Reuben's Delicatessen on Madison Avenue for a corned-beef sandwich and a hamburger, respectively, both of us laughing all the way at Saul's creation, his "wordless living novel." His friend rose to fame and fulfilled his spiritual needs as well as clearing all his debts. Saul, beaming, whispered, "I'm glad for your sake too, kid."

# VI.

## A Close Call

*I*n December of 1987, at our annual pre-Christmas dinner, Lois Wallace, agent and friend, asked if I'd seen the next month's *Vanity Fair*. "You really should take a look."

"That's what everyone tells me."

"There's a cover story about Andrew Wylie in it."

"I don't want to read about Andrew Wylie."

She reached into her tote bag. "I brought you an advance copy."

"I don't want it."

A week or so later, when the January issue hit the newsstands, Saul phoned. "Have you heard of an agent named Andrew Wylie?"

"Everyone keeps asking me that. What is it with this guy?"

"Adam just called me up. There's a piece in *Vanity Fair*. It says this Wylie spit on my book, on *More Die of Heartbreak*."

"So that's it! I love it. Everybody's been telling me to read the article, but nobody dared tell me why! Forget it. Forget him. Everyone knows about Andrew Wylie."

> *Half a dozen literary types gather for dinner in Greenwich Village. One is Hanif Kureishi . . . another is Andrew Wylie, literary agent. . . . Kureishi happens to have a copy of Saul Bellow's new novel,* More Die of Heartbreak, *which he puts on the table.*
>
> *"How can you read that?" Wylie sneers. "That book is utter drivel. I spit on that book."*
>
> *At which point, Wylie spits on the book.*
>
> *The book remains on the table, bespat, through dinner. Until Wylie, at the end of the meal, finishes one of the nonfilter cigarettes he chain-smokes and stubs out the butt on it."*
>
> —*Vanity Fair*, January 1988

I called Lois.

"I don't have to worry about Wylie. This guy should only spit on all our clients' books."

Tony Zwicker was chair of the National Arts Club Literary Committee in 1977, when Saul was awarded its gold medal. A friend ever since, she invited me to a dinner party, early in 1980, in honor of her dear friend and compatriot the Swiss writer Max Frisch. Among other guests at the table were John Leonard, former editor of The New York Times Book Review and then reviewer for the daily edition, an admirer of Frisch's work, and a recent college graduate whose passion for books led him to establish his own rare books and manuscripts enterprise.

The subject of when and where and how Tony and I met came up. Max began to relate a Nobel Prize story of his own. On October 21, 1976, he's at home. The phone rings. It's a Swedish journalist, who brings him good news: He is on the shortlist for the Nobel Prize in literature this year, the winner to be announced at 1:00 P.M. in Stockholm. Would he please stand by for a call? Max lay down on his bed beside the phone: Would he accept? What would he do with the money? Give it all to Amnesty International! That settled, he napped until awakened by the phone. He instantly picked up the receiver. It was the Swedish journalist: "The Nobel Prize has been awarded to Saul Bellow. Would you write a thousand-word piece about the author for our paper?"

John Leonard commented that The New York Times had called him for the same reason, and his piece appeared on the Saturday edition's editorial page.

The book dealer's ears pricked up. He leaned over and told me that he had written some short stories and was also interested in Bellow's work: books, manuscripts, papers. We met again at my office some months later, just after The Viking Press, at my request, delivered numerous packets of "foul matter" (publisher's lingo for original manuscripts, galleys, proofs, etc.) for various Bellow titles, the sight of which made the dealer's eyes light up a thousand watts. He looked at a smallish packet. "This alone is worth at least five figures. If there's all this material and much more at Bellow's home and office, this collection should be worth a serious sum."

I immediately called Saul, and it was all news to him. "You mean all this junk is worth something? I could just produce more pages and pages in my own hand." An agreement was drawn up, and the dealer had his work cut out for him—and an opportunity to make a giant step in his career toward the Big Time. After a while, however, it became clear that "biggety-big bucks" was just pie in the sky. The contract was terminated, and we engaged another dealer.

The next dealer, solid, practical, down-to-earth, professional, was honored to have been chosen and immediately explained the difficulties of the market. "The archive is not an integral collection. A goodly if not major portion is at the University of Chicago, a gift from Saul some years ago." Therefore, morally, historically, for posterity, the dealer felt that the collection belonged with the other half.

By now the project was getting on in years, without a sale. What about an auction for one title? I called Saul and offered the suggestion, which he thought a good idea, and so did the dealer, who then contacted the two most prominent houses. Christie's wasn't interested, Sotheby's was very interested. An agreement was drawn up, and the auction for Mr. Sammler's Planet was set for Tuesday, June 7, 1988, with a reserve price of $60,000.

A Sotheby's armored truck transported the collection (notebooks, holographs, type manuscripts, galley copies), and the archive was put on exhibit for a week before the big day. Rita Reif, the auction reporter for The New York

*Times*, was going to cover the event. David Reddin, from Sotheby's, was interviewed on National Public Radio. (Not long before, Andy Warhol's estate had been auctioned famously at Sotheby's.) Everyone was excited. Never before had there been such an auction for a living author's work.

A couple of days before the auction, Saul had rung me up. Adam transmitted the message from the first dealer we had used—they were now friends—that the auction was a bad idea.

The auction proceeded, the room was full. I was there, sitting in the back to see the whole thing.

Adam and Rachel and that first dealer were seated toward the front, as was Andreas Brown, owner of the legendary Gotham Book Mart. Forty minutes into the auction, up comes the Bellow. God, please let it at least go for the reserve. Then, for the first time, the possibility occurred to me: What if it doesn't sell?

David Reddin called, "Saul Bellow, *Mr. Sammler's Planet*. We have a reserve of sixty. I'm going to start at twenty-five."

And he did. "Twenty-five, thirty! Thirty-five, forty! Forty-five, fifty!" His hands alternated from one end of the room to the other. "Fifty-five, sixty! Final warning! Sixty!" Sold to Andy Brown! Amen.

I went immediately to the hall phone, to call Saul in Vermont. Harvey Ginsberg, Saul's editor, first at Harper & Row, now at Morrow, looked at me on the way out. "Did you see anything? I couldn't see anybody!" Actually, I didn't either. It all went pretty fast.

Andy Brown and two anonymous donors had bought the collection in time for Saul's seventy-third birthday, three days thereafter, and, in honor of the late Sam Goldberg, a mutual friend, were donating it as a gift to The New York Public Library.

*The New York Times* ran the story the next day, headlined: BELLOW PAPERS BRING A RECORD AT AUCTION. "For once I am speechless," said Dr. Lola Szladits of the Public Library's Berg Collection. "*Mr. Sammler's Planet* is Mr. Bellow's most important work, and I am ecstatic that it is part of the collection. Especially because New York City is where Mr. Sammler lives." Manuscripts and notebooks and papers would be placed on view for one month in the reading room of the Berg Collection.

They were on exhibit when the author read at the 92nd Street Y Poetry Center four months later, his first appearance there in decades. Saul inaugurated the Center's fiftieth-anniversary season on October 10, 1988, to a standing-room-only audience, even the seats onstage left just enough room for the podium and speaker.

Saul was introduced by none other than Lola Szladits.

Saul called a few months later. "Why don't we auction something else?"

In November of 1988, Saul was to appear at the Houston Book Fair, and the next day, at a book fair in Saint Louis. I'd never been to Houston, and the people with whom I was arranging things kept urging me: Are you coming? Are you coming? We can get you a private tour of the Menil Collection. Someone will take you to see it. That's some museum: Magritte, De Chirico, Duchamp, Picasso, African, medieval, Byzantine art.

I was kind of flush then, courtesy of *The Closing of the American Mind*, and I'd gotten this bright idea I wanted a little adventure. I called Saul and asked him if he would welcome my company to Houston. "That's very sporting of you, to spend your commission like that."

I called United Airlines to connect with his Chicago flight on Saturday morning. I'd fly from La Guardia to O'Hare, switch to first class (Saul had a first-class ticket), and we'd fly on to Houston together.

All excited, I got up very early and took a cab to La Guardia. I have plenty of time, I'm relaxed. I get to the terminal, look on the screen for the gate number. Where's the gate for Chicago? I walk to the very last gate, I look at the screen again, and it registers on me that all it shows is Orlando, West Palm Beach, Miami. Miami! I'm at Eastern Airlines! (The next month, I was going to Palm Beach, Florida, with Eastern. That Bloom royalty period was very nice.)

There goes my luxurious, leisurely, don't-get-overexcited trip. I'm running, running, running the length of the terminal. I'm thinking: Oh, this is it. I've missed the flight. I'm not going to make the connection to Houston! There was only one flight. I'm sweating bullets, my heart is racing, I can't believe it. I open my ticket and indeed there it is: United Airlines. The United terminal is a block and a half down the road.

I'm off and running again with my heavy suitcase. My hair's all wet and raggy, I'm a wreck, and I'm ready to throw up. What a mess!

If the flight hadn't been delayed fifteen minutes, I might not have made it.

We land at O'Hare, one of the biggest airports in the world, a maze of concourses and conveyors. The plane to Houston is on Concourse F, and I am on Concourse B. So I go downstairs and I get on a conveyor and then I have to get on another conveyor and another and another. I'm huffing and puffing. I finally get on the plane. There's Saul, sitting in the first row of first class and in my window seat, not his aisle seat. He looks up from his book. "You look like you've been running." I sit down, strap in, and we take off.

The first-class flight attendant comes over. "Ms. Bellow, what would you like to drink?" . . . "Mr. Wasserman, what will you have?"

Saul smiles at me. "Well, it's okay." The whole trip, he was called Mr. Wasserman and I was called Ms. Bellow.

He hands me a surprise, an honor, an unexpected gift: a Xerox of the first handwritten draft of *The Bellarosa Connection*. My first look at the manuscript, and it's finished!

Yoiks! I have only two-plus hours to read it, with the author sitting right next to me—and I have to make out his handwriting. That was my trip.

Saul took out a book to read and looked over at me from time to time. You have to be sincere. You have to be specific with Saul. You can't get away with a general impression. You can't just say, I think it's terrific! He can tell. "What about that? And what about this?" He can tell if you got it.

I came to the last page. "Zero to the bone"—as best expressed by Emily Dickinson. Incredible, important, stirring, powerful.

He relaxed.

In 102 pages, Saul Bellow addresses the Holocaust of Nazi-occupied Europe and the Americanization of refugees and the succeeding generation. In a sentence, in a word, more is said than volumes and volumes, fiction and non-fiction, written.

For instance:

> "I was at the *bar of paternal judgment* again, charged with American puerility . . . . Surviving-Fonstein, with all the furies of Europe at his back, made me look bad."

> "Some camps were run in a *burlesque* style. . . . Billy Rose wasn't the only one in show biz . . . the Germans did it too."

> "I had concluded long ago that the Chosen were chosen to read God's mind. Over the millennia, this turned out to be a zero-sum game."

> "If sleep is forgetting, forgetting is also sleep, and sleep is to consciousness what death is to life."

We were picked up at the Houston airport by a cardiologist, whose wife was managing the book fair. The doctor kept saying, "My wife asked if you're going to the Menil."

As we checked in at the Four Seasons Hotel, we noticed a lot of FBI men and security guards around the reception desk. It turned out George Bush was coming the next day, to vote for himself on Tuesday. They were staking out the joint. I went to my room, Saul went to his room. It was something like two-thirty in the afternoon, one hour earlier than New York time. I really wanted to go to that Menil.

Saul rang. "What are you doing?"

"Remember the doctor mentioning the Menil museum? Would you like to go?"

"Do *you* want to go? It's up to you. Did you come here to see me? Or did you come here for the Menil?"

You, you.

I met him downstairs in the coffee shop at about four, all the time thinking: Ooh, I really wanted to go to the Menil. . . . Well, next time.

At tea, he gave me an update on the goings-on of all his relatives. That's when I asked him if he would ever want to write a novel about his family. "Would I ever want to! But I would get killed for writing the most anti-Semitic novel ever written." We laughed so hard.

Then, out on the terrace, he told me how life was for him. I knew that was what he wanted, what he'd meant when he said, "That's very sporting of you to come." He was happy for the opportunity to talk with me in private about his entire life and what was happening with him, personally. It was the first time we had a talk since his new life had begun.

Two hours later, we were driven to this huge auditorium, almost airplane-hangar size, where the Jewish Book Fair was held. The house was packed. Standing room only. It was a Saturday night, obviously, the audience was there to have a good time, to be entertained. Saul gave this very erudite, heavy, major speech he'd been developing, on what it means for him to be an American and a Jew and a novelist. The woman in front of me took her compact out of her pocketbook and started to fix her face. Our cardiologist turned out to be deaf; sitting in the first row, he was madly cupping his ear. Everybody was getting restless as the delivery ran well over an hour. I looked around at all the faces. They wanted laughs. Saul was absolutely brilliant. What he said would have been riveting on a weekday at a philosophical, theological seminar.

When it was over, he received loud applause. Now on to the Houston Galleria, where a gala reception was to be held at the Tiffany store owned by the chairman of the book fair committee. We were driven to the mall by the deaf doctor. He said to Saul, in the passenger seat, "That was a very interesting talk. I don't think I got all of it. How come you chose to speak on that subject? I'm not sure that I was able to follow you, completely." I cringed in the backseat: Saul must have been having a fit, and rightly so.

We arrived at the Galleria, on the mezzanine over-looking a rink with ice-skaters and canned music. Tiffany's—the entire shop—was opened especially for the occasion and surrounded inside and out by security guards, some of them from the Houston Police Department's SWAT team. I loved looking all around. The food was fabulous, served by waiters on huge silver platters; the drinks flowed; the dessert table, luscious, featured rich chocolate whipped-cream cakes. The huge crowd was called to attention by the Tiffany owner, who gave a short speech and made a presentation to Saul of an enormous crystal Tiffany prism with a sterling-silver plate that was inscribed to mark the occasion. I was standing next to him and was introduced as Saul Bellow's literary agent. That's when Saul added, "My coach, manager, and trainer."

It might have been the first time a New York agent came to Houston with a client, they seemed to get such a kick out of my being there. They presented me with a Tiffany silk scarf, so beautiful, and just the right colors for the outfit I was wearing.

At the reception, the first on the greeting line said, "Mr. Herzog, it's a great pleasure to meet you." And the next:

"It's a great pleasure to meet you, Mr. Bellow. Your speech went right over my head, I couldn't understand a word."

Before dawn on Sunday, I rose and headed back to New York. Saul went on to Missouri to deliver the same address at the Saint Louis Book Fair.

A nephew of a good friend, lawyer extraordinaire Ed Klagsbrun, had been killed as he celebrated his twenty-fourth birthday the previous January. The murder made headlines as "The Karate Killer Case." Herb and Emilie Klagsbrun wanted to set up an appropriate memorial to their son at an annual seminar on "Writing and Moral Vision" at Connecticut College, Danny's alma mater.

Saul agreed to inaugurate the series. "I'll give them the Jewish speech," he said.

"Saul, are you sure it's appropriate? Isn't it supposed to be on Writing and Moral Vision?" I even went back to the archive and got a piece he had written in 1963 for the *Atlantic Monthly*, called "Morality and Literature." I called him up.

"No, no, that's an old piece, that was in '63. What's the matter with my Jewish speech? I rewrote the speech, I revised it, I fixed it up."

So I hired a NY RADIO car ("You know our name. You know our number"), and we drove up to New London and went into the lounge to have a drink with Danny's father, Herb, and his uncle Ed, and Blanche Boyd, head of the English Department.

Herb: "I'm so moved and so honored that you would come like this for Danny."

Saul: "Your son's name was Daniel? My son's name is Daniel."

Herb said, "How old is your Danny?"

"Twenty-five."

"Danny would have been twenty-five." Total frozen silence. It was extremely moving, both men just completely silent.

Blanche started talking about how she's not drinking anymore, about growing up in Tennessee, about life in the South. She mentioned about a zillion Christian things.

Saul pulled me aside. "My Jewish speech is going to go down real big here!"

Then we went to dinner at the president's house. There was not a scintilla of Jewishness. Of course, Saul picked up on that very quickly. He excused himself and went to the bathroom. After a while, the president went after him, came back, and said, "Mr. Bellow is having tachycardia!" (He was having a huge anxiety attack, because he feared he had the wrong speech and he was about to give it.) He needed to take his pills.

At the auditorium, Saul sat on the stage, then Blanche came to the podium. "This is going to be the inaugural of an annual seminar, because Danny was very interested in writing and in morality. We have Saul Bellow, the Nobel Prize winner." I almost didn't want to look. I saw Saul had his handkerchief out.

"I have the great honor of giving the inaugural speech on 'Writing and Moral Vision,' and I realize that I have never spoken about what it is to be a Jewish-American writer, my identity, so this is the first time that I'm speaking on this, and this has to do with morality." It was extraordinary, actually. He talked about what it meant to be a Jewish novelist: "For some people you're too Jewish. For some you're not Jewish enough. . . ." At the end, he got a standing ovation!

(Blanche Boyd was a panelist at a southern writers' conference I had attended in Charleston one year. Speaking about the difference/similarity between Christian families and Jewish families—she had frequently attended dinners with each—she made the observation: Both have tales of tragedy and woe to tell around the table. The difference is the Christian families laugh and laugh at the sad stories; the Jewish families cry.)

Once again, Saul Bellow was a promising young writer. He began work on a new novel, *A Case of Love*, and began sending me pages.

So I was both surprised and delighted when I received an envelope from Vermont—where Saul and Janis, now living together, were taking a winter holiday—with a new long story, "A Theft."

*Esquire* was the choice for first submission. Times had changed. Magazines were devoting less and less space to fiction, even for Bellow. "A Theft"'s length fit the story perfectly; it could not be cut.

Earlier in the decade, the *Atlantic Monthly* had published the eponymous story of his collection *Him with His Foot in His Mouth*. The *Atlantic's* William Whitworth wanted very much to publish Saul again, but not only did he cite the same predicament as *Esquire* (and indeed most national magazines); he added that were "Him with His Foot in His Mouth"—shorter than "A Theft"—submitted now, he wouldn't be able to publish it for reasons of length.

"What do they mean? What do they mean, too long? That's just the reason they gave you."

Crisis. With each new work, Saul is a new writer, writing his first novel, his first short story. A rejection is a rejection is a rejection.

What to do? I certainly didn't want to risk another turndown. Implicit in what Saul was saying to me was that he couldn't take another rejection like that. Who could blame him?

Why not a paperback original? Just right for an odd-size manuscript, too short for a hardcover book and too long for magazines.

From *The Adventures of Augie March* (1953) through *To Jerusalem and Back* (1976), Viking had been Saul's hardback publisher. Peter Mayer, when at Avon, bought *Humboldt's Gift*, which became a huge paperback best-seller, as well as the earlier titles. Now Peter was CEO at Viking Penguin, and it seemed right for a paperback original to go to him there. The launch of the original paperback novella received much attention in the press. A new idea, a new market.

Publication of *A Theft* marked important firsts. Not only was it the first time a major American literary figure chose to be published originally in paperback, but what's more, the central character, strong, passionate, indomitable Clara Velde, is the first woman protagonist of a Bellow book. It is not uninteresting to note that *A Theft* follows publication, two years earlier, of the tenth Bellow novel, *More Die of Heartbreak*, which drew criticism from certain reviewers for being misogynistic.

Highly acclaimed, widely reviewed, *A Theft* was published in March 1989, followed by *The Bellarosa Connection* in October 1989. Two novellas, written and published in the same year: a considerable achievement.

In September, Saul and Janis married.

While continuing to work on the full-length novel, Saul wrote a short story, "Something to Remember Me By," published in *Esquire* in 1992 and a winner of a National Magazine Fiction Award.

Simultaneously with *A Case of Love*, pages for yet another novel, *All Marbles Still Accounted For*, started coming. Saul was writing two novels virtually in tandem, until it became apparent that *All Marbles Still Accounted For* wanted his full attention and he continued working toward its completion.


Roger W. Straus and Saul Bellow are members of a mutual admiration society. In July 1991, Isaac Bashevis Singer died. Roger called. "Now can I be Saul Bellow's publisher?"—a question he had asked five years earlier, after Bernard Malamud's passing, and, again, after Philip Roth left.

A couple of years passed. I'm having lunch one day with Roger. "Did you handle the film contract for *Zelig*? I got Susan Sontag five thousand dollars for her part. What did you get for Bellow?"

"I got five thousand dollars."

"And I got royalties for her. Did you get royalties for him?"

I thought he was boasting, and didn't say anything.

Late in 1993, I called Saul, and Janis answered the phone. She was doing a roundup of taxes for the year's return.

"Do you have the number for the accounting department at Warner Brothers? Saul didn't get his annual 1099 form for *Zelig* royalties."

Suddenly I hear Saul in the background. "What's that? Who's that?"

"It's Harriet, I'm asking her about the 1099 form for *Zelig*."

"Never mind, never mind, we'll find it ourselves!"

Oops, Janis let the cat out of the bag. Saul's been getting royalties directly.

In all these years, Saul has been steadily writing short nonfiction—articles, lectures, reportage, tributes, essays, criticism, thought pieces—on a wide range of subjects: "The Yellow Kid," FDR, Khrushchev, the White House, Dostoevsky, the Information Revolution, the Camp David Accord, Mozart, Paris, Tuscany, the Irùn-Madrid Express Railroad, NewYork, all of which I have read and seen in the aggregate. Few people, including Saul him-self, were aware of the number and substance of the contributions published here and there and every-where.

It seemed time to collect them. Saul had recently pub-lished two novellas and a number of stories, and he was writing a full-length novel, full-time. Why not such a collection in the year or two before the new novel would be finished and brought out?

While Saul was in Paris for an extended stay, I made encouraging calls with all my reasons. Saul at first was resistant. Ever the self-improver, he would of course want to revise all the pieces from 1948 to date. In his judgment, they were of uneven quality. Such a collec-tion would appear to be a kind of filler because there was nothing else—sometimes the case with such col-lections.

Okay, how about this: Saul would select only those pieces he wished to be included, and organize them, which would take minimal time away from work on the novel. I would take care of copyrights, assignments, per-missions, etc. Marge Horvitz, copy editor, would be included in the contract.

Persistent persuasion paid off. Saul agreed only on con-dition that he could arrange the collection in other than chronological order (brilliant—of course!) and write a preface. When he sat down and read the pieces again, made his selections, and called in the perfect title—*It All Adds Up: From the Dim Past to the Uncertain Future*—I knew that he, too, was now pleased.

In 1992, the year of Barley Alison's death, Allan Bloom's luck ran out. He had tested his health mightily. He suffered from coronary artery disease and a damaged muscle following a serious heart attack, yet he chain-smoked and ate anything he pleased. His cholesterol level, something unbelievable—"2000," he joked (I think?)—was controlled by experimental medication from the National Institutes of Health. Once, in his dining room, I watched him with the butter, the bacon, the cream, the Gauloise. I suggested that maybe he should at least cut down on the cigarettes. There wasn't much else he could do to help himself. He said he didn't care. He enjoyed his cigarettes, his food. He wasn't going to give up his pleasures. I understood.

Allan fell ill with Guillain-Barré, a totally debilitating disease. He wrote his next book as he slowly and bravely recuperated, only to be struck down again, by liver failure, just as he finished.

He lay in a coma in the hospital, close to death.

I told Saul and Nathan Tarcov, Allan's executor, "When you go visit him, speak close to his ear. Tell him that his new book is in the catalog and will appear in the spring." The new book was *Love and Friendship*.

Nathan called me, excited. He had spoken clearly in Allan's ear. Allan woke up. "My book is in the catalog?"

He had two days of consciousness, then died on October 8, 1992, at the age of fifty-seven.

Saul stayed in Chicago for only one semester after his friend was gone. He accepted an offer from John Silber, the president of Boston University, to join the University Professors Program. Janis Bellow was to teach two classes. Allan had been her adviser but died before she defended her thesis. Saul went with her to her oral defense.

Among the luminaries at the annual Literary Lights Award fund-raising dinner on March 13, 1994, for the Boston Public Library, the oldest public library in the country, was Saul Bellow, who delivered opening remarks and himself received an award.

Preceding this ceremony by days was a column in the *Boston Globe* that began by stating that the chairman of the Literary Lights Committee had been asked to uninvite Saul as honored guest. This had been prompted by an article by Brent Staples in *The New York Times Magazine* a month earlier, which was preceded by an article in *The New Yorker* by Alfred Kazin, itself prompted by a misleading quote in a 1988 *New York Times Magazine* cover story by James Atlas—the unfortunate root of all of which may be traced back almost thirty years.

An excerpt from Staples's memoir, *Parallel Times: Growing Up Black and White*, appeared in *The Times Magazine* on February 6. It was described by Sarah Lyall in her "Book Notes" column days later: Mr. Staples, when a young graduate student, "felt horribly conflicted about Mr. Bellow's work. On the one hand, he considers the novelist a hero, a dazzlingly gifted writer. On the other hand, as a young Black man, Mr. Staples was frustrated and aggrieved by Mr. Bellow's characters' ugly descriptions of Blacks. In a particularly vivid passage, Mr. Staples, now an editor for the *Times*, relates how he once followed Mr. Bellow with a wild fantasy about confronting him, although he abandoned the idea."

Coincidentally, that same month, a comment reportedly made by Saul Bellow in a 1988 interview was suddenly and mistakenly interpreted by Kazin in *The New Yorker*.

For his part, Mr. Kazin said, the comment "made his heart sink."

Kazin's opinion was based on a misleading quote in Atlas's 1988 *Times Magazine* article on Allan Bloom, for which Saul had been interviewed. The quote—"Who is the Tolstoy of the Zulus? The Proust of the Papuans?"— appeared to have been spoken by Saul directly to Atlas during that interview, which it was not.

It was taken out of context from a similar remark, which, Saul recalls in a March 10, 1994, *New York Times* op-ed piece, he made in a telephone interview years before, speaking of the distinction between preliterate and literate societies. Immediately after that telephone interview, he remembered that there was a Zulu novel, *Shaka*, by Thomas Mfolo, published in the early 1930s, which he read in translation at the time—"a profoundly, unbearably tragic book." At college, Saul, an anthropology major, was a student of the famous Africanologist, M. J. Herskovitz. The subject of his senior thesis was "France and the African Slave Trade."

Saul goes on to ask, "Why did my remarks throw so many people into fits of righteousness and ecstasies of rage? France gave us one Proust and only one. There is no Bulgarian Proust. Have I offended the Bulgarians, too? We, for that matter, have no Proust, either. My critics, many of whom cannot locate Papua New Guinea on a map, want to convict me of contempt for multiculturalism and defamation of the Third World."

The *Boston Globe* column before the Literary Lights dinner made reference to "Brent Staples lacerating Bellow for his demeaning and stereotyped depiction of Black characters in his novels. . . . Staples, a former doctoral candidate at the University of Chicago, where Bellow taught before joining the faculty at Boston University, slammed Bellow for writing Black characters into his novels who were frightening, hypersexualized and cruel. . . . The criticisms were not entirely new. Bellow has been controversial among Black scholars for decades."

Claude Brown, author of *Manchild in the Promised Land*, had a rather visceral reaction to *Mr. Sammler's Planet*. He said, for example, that he wouldn't use the pages of the novel as toilet paper.

The genesis of all this was the tall black man in the camel coat on the Broadway bus who sees Mr. Sammler observing him as he picks pockets, gets off at his stop, follows Mr. Sammler, and intimidates him by exposing himself.

Saul, who had trepidations of protestors disrupting the fund-raiser, was confounded by the Staples piece. He said to me, "There's this young man in Chicago who was stalking me. He never came to see me. Why didn't he come up to see me? We could have had some interesting discussions. If he wanted to come into my class, he'd have been welcome. He didn't have to stalk me. It would have been so much more interesting to talk."

Saul is as deeply emotional as he is highly intellectual and cerebral, an uncommon combination. He seems to need that stimulation to be constantly charged all the time: new adventures and exchanges of new ideas. Perhaps this accounts for the number and duration of his marriages.

Saul spoke for himself in the op-ed piece: "Preliterate societies have their own kind of wisdoms, and primitive Papuans probably have a better grasp of their myths than most educated Americans have of their own literature. But without years of study, we cannot begin to understand a culture very different from our own. The fair thing, therefore, is to make allowance for what we outsiders cannot hope to fathom in another society, and grant that, as members of the same species, primitive men are as mysterious or as monstrous as any other branch of humankind."

*Henderson the Rain King*, Saul's fifth novel, has three major characters, black—Romilayu, Dahfu, and Itelo—"with the wisdom of life" for which the protagonist, Eugene Henderson, has been longing.

The characters in Saul's novels are men and women,

Gentiles and Jews, blacks and whites. There are good ones, there are bad ones, and some of them are "frightening, hypersexualized and cruel."

Toward the end of the fifties, Ralph Ellison and Saul roomed together in Tivoli, New York, when they were teaching at Bard. "We did have literary company in Dutchess County. Ralph and I in our slummy mansion could not entertain for more prosperous literary squires. . . . No one in our group was altogether free from pride. . . . The presence of a Jew or a Negro in any group is apt to promote a sense of superiority in those who—whatever else—are neither Jews nor Negroes."*

In *Compton's Living Encyclopedia*, the Bellow entry states: "Although he is frequently labeled a Jewish writer, the classification belies Saul Bellow's concern with basic human dilemmas, a preoccupation that transcends ethnic and religious boundaries. Bellow's books . . . reflect his belief that one of the writer's chief functions is to remind people of their common humanity."

One scene in one novel published almost three decades ago escalated into such grotesque misunderstanding.

———

*From Saul Bellow's preface to *The Collected Essays of Ralph Ellison* (New York: Modern Library, 1995).

On Thanksgiving Day, 1994, on the island of Saint Martin, Saul ate a toxic fish, developed double pneumonia, and had to be airlifted to Boston University Medical Center, where he was put under anesthesia and on a respirator. He was in intensive care for weeks, battling for his life. Adam was the first to inform me, the Monday after the big holiday weekend.

I had spoken to Saul in the Caribbean on Wednesday. He was staying at Flamboyant Beach Villas, working on his novel-in-progress, *All Marbles Still Accounted For*. The last section takes place in New Guinea, and he needed a tropical clime. He and Janis planned to be there for the month of November. It was hard to use the phone, as they were staying in someone's lodging house and there were kids shouting and running around. Adam called me and said, "Can you call my father? He says he hasn't heard from you."

I phoned and asked Saul what he would do for Thanksgiving. "After I write, we sit on the beach and read Shakespeare. *The Tempest*, *A Midsummer Night's Dream*. Can you send me some Shakespeare? And if you want, you can send me a little treat." I knew the treat he meant was chocolate and caramels, his favorites. I got the books at Barnes & Noble, included chocolate turkeys and caramels, and sent the packet off Federal Express.

Before we hung up: "Can you call Adam and find out how he is?"

On Monday, back in my office, I returned from a lunch date and heard Adam's voice on my machine, telling me not to try to reach his father in the Caribbean. He had been flown to Boston Hospital on Friday, critically ill.

I thought everything was okay. Adam left a message saying Saul had "turned a corner." Then Janis's father called me from Toronto. "Janis asked me to call. Saul is a very, very sick man. We have to pray for him. He's in a very bad way." Saul's father-in-law is a psychiatrist. When a psychiatrist says that you have to pray, I thought, that's the end. So I called Adam at home, and he said he was going up the next day. He called me Tuesday from the hospital and said that Saul had had a bad night but was sitting up and reading *The New York Times* and discussing an op-ed piece with him.

Wednesday, it was a different story. Adam reported that Saul had had another bad night, and it wasn't looking good at all. One lung was not working, and the other was having difficulties. The doctors thought Saul's condition was caused by a quinine overload, because they had a hard time regulating his heartbeat.

By Thursday, his physician put him on a respirator to let his body rest and give it sufficient oxygen. Instead of morphine, his great-niece Rachel, an anesthesiology resident at the University of Cincinnati Hospital, recommended a new kind of anesthesia.

On Friday morning, his condition remained unchanged. Adam called me from the hallway of the hospital. "Daniel's here too, and he says hi!" I asked Adam for permission to get hold of the infectious-diseases specialist who had prescribed exactly the antibiotic that saved my life when I got that staph infection. At least professional would be talking to professional. I got his permission.

Then Greg called from Redwood City and bawled me out.

"You're not to call that specialist. We are only going to have one line here. I'm the oldest, and I'm in charge. I'm in touch with the infectious-diseases doctor and Saul's primary doctor. You are not to interfere."

"Okay, sure." Then I said, "I'd like to come this weekend."

"No. You are not to come this weekend."

Before I could call off my doctor, he called me.

"Saul Bellow the writer?" He was very impressed. When I told him they hadn't yet discovered the source, he said that wasn't unusual, it could be hundreds of different kinds of bacteria. A wide-spectrum antibiotic, he confirmed, was the best course. I immediately called Adam and told him, and he felt better.

Saul's friend Walter Pozen called. "Janis [in Boston] asked her father [in Toronto] to call me [in Washington] to call you [in New York] to ask if you could advance a sum to cover the bills at the beginning of the month. If you can't do it, I'll do it."

I told him that on November 19 I had deposited two checks into Saul's account that would more than cover it. "Fine."

Then one phone call after another, including one asking who had power of attorney. (In fact, Saul had once given me power of attorney, but limited only to one trip abroad.) A grim Friday.

Monday, Greg called to say there was some slight improvement. He apologized for having raised his voice. I told him I understood.

Janis, alas, may have misunderstood and thought the boys were usurping her authority. They all expressed to me their appreciation of her care and attention to their father.

Saul rallied more and more every day. All his sons wanted to be there when he opened his eyes. When he did, they were. "A fourteen-year-old strong boy couldn't pull through the way Saul Bellow has," his chief attending physician proclaimed in awe.

Saul's recovery, miraculous as it was, was slow and debilitating. The toxins affected his nervous system as well as other systems. Lots of physical therapy was required. But characteristically, he bounced back at the earliest possible moment: testing out his driving skills by making a trip by car with Janis from Boston to his Vermont home and back within weeks of his hospitalization, conducting classes in his living room, and even giving an address at BU that had been scheduled way before the illness.

At the top and back of his mind all the while, no doubt, was the almost Biblical test with a toxic fish, from which he emerged triumphant, just at the approach of his eightieth birthday in June: Another living Saul Bellow story.

Day before Memorial Day weekend, a message appeared on my answering machine "for Harriet Wasserman about Mr. Bellow from Andrew Wylie. You can reach me at the Hamptons over the weekend at 516 . . . or on Tuesday in the office."

The week before, I had been speaking to Wendy Weil, the artist Saul Steinberg's agent. Penguin was preparing to bring out a uniform edition of all the Saul Bellow novels in the Penguin Twentieth-Century American Classics series.

Saul was to select the cover art. Then he got sick. Penguin had to go ahead; they planned to do three titles a year.

"Saul, what if I suggest photographs for each title? I'd love to do that." He agreed. So I made up a list of suggestions for his approval. For example: *Seize the Day*—the Ansonia Hotel around Broadway, *Augie March*—the Chicago el or Wabash Avenue in the twenties or thirties, *Henderson the Rain King*—a lion on the African plain.

Penguin found the perfect photograph for each.

However, for *Henderson the Rain King*, Saul wanted to use an illustration that Steinberg had given him as a gift. (Saul wrote *Henderson* before he'd ever been to Africa. After publication, the leader of Kenya invited Saul as his guest.) The two Sauls had met coincidentally in Africa. They came toward each other on a dirt road.

"Saul?"

"Saul?"

So Bellow and Steinberg continued on together.

I asked Saul B. to send me the Saul S. illustration.

"It's all framed. Why don't you call Saul Steinberg?" I did, and he didn't have a reproducible copy.

So I called his agent. "Oh, I don't represent him anymore. He went with Andrew Wylie," Wendy Weil said.

And I said, Oh, no! That's something I don't have to worry about. Andrew Wylie once spit on *More Die of*

*Heartbreak* and snuffed out his cigarette in the spittle.

Thus, when Wylie called me the next weekend, I thought it had to do with the Saul Steinberg illustration.

Still, I called Wylie back reluctantly. The conversation went something like this:

"I've spoken with Saul Bellow, and I want to buy his backlist from Russell & Volkening and handle his foreign rights."* He said your relationship both as an agent and as a friend was sacrosanct. If it's all right with you, it's all right with him," he said. "I'd like to come and talk to you for about an hour."

"Didn't you spit on *More Die of Heartbreak* and snuff your cigarette out in the spittle?"

"Oh, no, that's not true."

---

*__What's backlist?__ Those S. Bellow books for which contracts were negotiated from 1948 through 1972 by Henry Volkening and until 1981 by yours truly in the employ of R&V: Nine titles at Viking, *The Adventures of Augie March* through *To Jerusalem and Back*; one title at Harper & Row, *The Dean's December*. For the life of each contract, R&V continues to receive its ten percent commission on earnings from sales by the U.S. publisher. As of opening of business Fall 1981, HWLA was appointed authorized agent to act in all matters with respect to these titles, such services performed as a courtesy, without commission (e.g., negotiating amendments to the old contracts, processing statements and payments, etc.) For all other rights, such as motion picture, dramatic, or translation, HWLA is compensated with its traditional commission.

__Foreign rights__ Translation into languages in countries throughout the world are usually negotiated for limited periods only, e.g., five, seven years. So that, upon expiration, all Bellow contracts for all old and new titles would be by Wylie contracts.

"Really? I've been representing him for more than twenty-five years."

He said, "I can do a better job than you can."

I said, "Well, that's a put-down. Come on, Andrew, you don't just want his backlist and his foreign rights—you want all of him."

"No, no. I'm willing to give you a signed letter. I've been handling a lot of estates lately."

"Saul Bellow isn't an estate, he's a living writer. You *sure* you didn't spit on his book?"

"I told you. I'll give you a signed letter."

"Would you give me a signed letter saying you didn't spit on his book?"

Pause.

"Well, you're going to retire soon. If Wylie has the backlist and foreign rights, whatever you have will be worth more to Wylie, and you'll get more."

"Wait a minute—what do you mean? I'm not planning to retire or sell my agency. Do you want to buy me out?"

"Maybe if the price is right. I'm in an aggressive and expansive mood."

I said, "You have more literary territory than Alexander the Great. And aggressive? I thought you were a pussy-cat."

"Only my daughter knows that."

"Why don't you go after somebody else? Why are you going after Bellow?"

"Oh, because he's the greatest writer."

"You sure you didn't spit on his book?"

"He's the greatest writer we have." And he quoted almost word for word Robert Towers's 1982 *New York Times Book Review* line about *The Dean's December*, saying, "Sentence by sentence, word by word, Saul Bellow is simply the greatest writer we have."

"Did you call him, or did he call you?"

"I called him."

"When?"

"Some months ago."

Oh, oh, oh . . . I realized Wylie was not coming to me at the beginning: he was coming to me at the end. He was not calling to ask me; he was calling to tell me. Absolutely flummoxed, I said, "Thank you very much for calling. This is all news to me. I haven't spoken to my client about it. Thank you." And I hung up.

The next day, I called Saul, to tell him about a substantial additional amount that I had just finalized in an ongoing negotiation for an existing backlist contract. He said, "That's nice." Then he said, "By the way, I hear you spoke to Mr. Wylie yesterday."

I said, "Yes. What was that all about?"

"He wants to buy my backlist and he tells me he can do much better for me on foreign rights too. Just hear me out on this."

"Saul, he spat on your book."

"Yeah, I know. I asked him about it. He said it wasn't true."

"Oh, sure, he's not going to tell you he did! Did he call you, or did you call him?"

"He called me."

"When?"

"The end of February. He called me up in Boston and asked to come see me. It's a free country. I said okay, come up to see me."

In early February, when Saul had come home from the hospital, I called his secretary and asked if he was making any appointments. Yes: twice a week, at his house.

"Good. Can you make an appointment for me? The last time I spoke with him was in the hospital, and he told me he'd love for me to come."

Then he called me up at the beginning of March. "I don't think we have anything to talk about that we can't talk about on the phone."

Aha! I'd been puzzled by his gruff voice at the time, but now the answer became clear.

I said, "Saul, you can do whatever you want, but there is no such thing as two agents."

"I told Wylie he'd have to sign a piece of paper for you."

"There's no such thing. There's one author and one agent. You don't divide up lists. You can only have one agent. Any one you want. If it's Wylie, fine. Geh gesunderheit!"* (All my life, I'd been dying to use that line.)

The whole summer went by, and not a word was mentioned again. Saul sent a new story to me, "By the St. Lawrence," which Esquire snapped up. We continued business as usual. I thought it was over. Until mid-September.

"Now, don't get excited. Hear me out on this. I really want you to consider this about the foreign rights and the backlist."

"Of course, do what you want to do. If you want to go with Andrew Wylie, that's fine. But he knows there is no such thing as dual agents, it just doesn't work that way."

"But he told me he'd sign a paper for you."

"I asked him instead to sign a letter saying he didn't spit on your book. It doesn't mean anything. If you think he can do a better job than me, fine, that's fine. But I have to know where I stand!"

"I'll think it over and let you know."

*Literally translated from Yiddish: Go in good health!

"I have the best clients in the world to serve. I have a business to run."

"I haven't made up my mind yet."

I called him during dinner Friday of the weekend before a reading scheduled for the 92nd Street Y. "Have you invited Andrew Wylie to your reading?"

Pause. To deny or not to deny.

"He called me up and asked me for tickets. So what."

"Saul, are you going to Andrew Wylie as your agent?"

"I told you, I haven't made up my mind. I'll let you know, when I think it over."

"I have to know where I stand!"

"I'm not going to speak to you if you raise your voice."

I hung up.

Saul called Ed, HWLA counsel, who acted as counsel for Saul as well, on other than agency matters.

Then Ed called me. "The poor guy. He hasn't made up his mind. Call him up. He thinks you're firing him. He thinks you're resigning."

"Oh, please, give me a break."

Monday, October 2, in town for the reading, Saul phoned. "Will Harriet accept a call from Mr. Bellow?" he asked my assistant.

I picked up the phone. "Oh, Saul. I really look forward to seeing you tonight. The reading's going to be wonderful!"

It was magnificent.

Rust Hills, fiction editor at *Esquire*, had published Saul from the January 1958 issue, with the story "Leaving the Yellow House," to the July 1995 summer fiction issue, with "By the St. Lawrence," Saul's latest story to date.

For Rust's own sixtieth birthday, he had called to tell me that what he wanted most for a present would be "dinner in Chicago with Saul Bellow." Did I think it was all right if he asked Saul? Saul was tickled. Rust and his wife, Joy Williams, flew to Chicago and had a memorable dinner.

Rust introduced Saul that night at the Y.

"In the accumulated work of any distinctive author, there is a context of voice and subject that creates a 'world,' and just as we can speak of 'Faulkner's World' and 'Hemingway's World' and 'the World of Henry James' and know what we're talking about—the sort of characters that inhabit that world, the system of values that operates in it—so too we can speak of 'Bellow's World' and know what we're talking about."

I called Saul the next morning, he told me he was still thinking things over.

Almost every other day after that, Ed called. "Harriet, I just had another call from Saul. He says he hasn't made up his mind yet."

"You don't get it. He has made up his mind already."

"You're wrong about that. Saul keeps saying, I don't know if I have an agent. Is she resigning? Is she firing me?"

Saul asked one time too many—on the twenty-fourth of October. It was like being zapped by an electrical prod.

I sat down and wrote him a fax. "Let's skip the chronology and go straight to a resolution. It is my understanding that you have dismissed me as your agent. It doesn't all add up that you keep asking if I'm resigning, if I'm firing you. . . ." I even quoted from the last sentence of Mr. Sammler's Planet: ". . . that we know, we know, we know . . ."

I did not hear from Saul again until a note in November, telling me that a new lawyer would be requesting that I gather all his material, contracts, etc. The lawyer asked for a meeting. I came to his office. He told me that Saul hadn't made up his mind yet, that he himself was a neutral third party, engaged to look over all my work and Wylie's proposition and advise Saul.

In early December, Saul is on the phone to me for the first time since I sent him the October fax. He's very friendly.

"How's your health?" My cue.

"How's your health?"

"Well, I'm going into the hospital for a gallbladder operation."

I sent flowers.

Saul recuperated and asked me to negotiate a contract with Viking Penguin for his collected short stories.

A week after that, the lawyer phoned and gave me the word. "Saul would like Andrew Wylie to handle his back-list and his foreign rights and for you to be his primary agent under Wylie's supervision."

I told him there was no such thing.

"Would you be willing to meet with Andrew Wylie?"

"I would rather meet you at the Forty-second Street and Eighth Avenue subway and clean the men's room toilet bowl with my tongue. Is that clear, or do you want me to be more specific?"

He said he'd tell Saul.

The lawyer called back on February 8. "Well, Saul has made up his mind. I hate to do this, it's the kind of call I hate to make, but he's going with Andrew Wylie."

My two new assistants were watching and listening. They had just entered this drama, and they were wide-eyed. I said, "Then I'm officially terminated."

"Yes. On behalf of Saul Bellow, you're officially terminated."

I hung up and said to my assistants, "I've been sacked!"

The next week, I got a call from Mary Tabor of *The New York Times*.

The following morning, Valentine's Day, this news item ran in the "Book Notes" column:

### BELLOW MAKES CHANGE

*After 25 years together, Saul Bellow is leaving his longtime literary agent, Harriet Wasserman, to join the growing group of writers flocking to sign up with Andrew Wylie, according to several people in the publishing world. Wylie, who recently signed Norman Mailer, Martin Amis and Pat Barker, has acquired the nickname "The Jackal." No one knows why, but one reason might be his capture of clients from other agents' lists. . . .*

Saul called me up noonish. "Did you see the paper? It's a lie, it's a lie."

I said, "It's a lie? You mean you haven't left me after twenty-five years? Andrew Wylie isn't your new agent?"

He offered a diversion. "Well, did you ever know a paper to tell the truth?"

"Saul, are you writing?"

"Yes."

"Write good. Bye-bye."

Half an hour later, his lawyer called me. "You know that article's absolutely not true?"

"Of course it's true! You officially terminated me on February 8." He declined my request to put it in writing.

"Oh, no, you misunderstood. I officially terminated you for the backlist and the foreign rights. You would still be Saul's primary agent, under the supervision of Andrew Wylie."

I sent him a fax. "For the sake of clarity and good order, I would be happy to receive and respond to any communications in writing."

What a turnaround from our first conversation. "I've heard many good things about you from a number of people."

"Name one."

"My client Adam Bellow."

Friday, a call from Mary Tabor. Her supervisor at the *Times* had responded to a call from Saul, who asked for a "correction." "You did tell me . . . ?"

"Yes, of course."

What a relief! That's all over. It's not only yesterday's news, it's the day before yesterday's news.

The following Tuesday, a second call. Mr. Bellow has just asked the executive editor for a "correction."

Now top brass was personally involved and wanted a complete and detailed report, to be prepared as if it were to run as a feature article.

The New York Times did not see fit to print.

In April 1996, a copy of a handwritten note by Saul to one of his foreign publishers appeared before my eyes, no doubt unbeknownst to Saul: "Harriet has cast me into outer darkness and no longer communicates with me, though there is unfinished business to do."

I knew he wished me to infer and carry out a final duty on his behalf.

In true Bellovian fashion, I was to fire myself.

After all, I represented him. If I didn't do it, who would?

An article in the August 11, 1996, issue of The New York Times Magazine, entitled "The Literary Agent as Zelig," refers to Saul's new agent. "Colleagues have noted his growing affinity for the estates of deceased writers like Italo Calvino and the backlists of aged authors like Bellow." Andrew Wylie is quoted. "They're cash cows, and everyone's happy to sit around and drink cups of milk. The trick is to turn them into cash bulls."

At the time of publication of *More Die of Heartbreak*, in June 1987, the *Times*'s Mervyn Rothstein, in a moving interview titled "Bellow on Love, Art and Identity," ended with a Saul Bellow quote: "Our humanity is in so many ways intact. Ordinary people can still see King Lear and weep."

Tom Victor, concerned about Saul Bellow's wattles and jowls at a session in 1984, put the lights on, went over to Saul, shoved the loose skin under his shirt collar, and tightened his tie, so fast Saul hardly realized what was going on before it was all over and Tom started shooting.

Saul's maternal grandfather in the old country.

Der 6jährige Saul Bellow mit seiner vollständigen Familie (Foto: Harriet Wassermann)

Saul Bellow erhält den Literatur-Nobelpreis 1976 (Foto: Harriet Wassermann)

Longtime German publisher, Kiepenheuer & Witsch, in honor of Saul Bellow's seventy-fifth birthday, June 10, 1990, printed a wonderful collage of photographs over the years on a huge poster. The two photos shown above, Saul at age six with his family (1921) and Saul receiving the Nobel Prize from the King of Sweden (1976), are credited to "(Foto: Harriet Wassermann) *sic*."

Saul receiving an honorary degree from Trinity College in
Dublin; behind him, poet Robert Lowell. (Phoned by an English
newspaper to verify the name of the man behind Saul Bellow,
Harriet Wasserman repeated the last name several times. The cap-
tion in the clipping read: "…behind him, Noel Coward.")

Photograph given to Harriet Wasserman by publisher Thomas H.
Guinzburg, son of Harold, late founder of The Viking Press. From
left to right Tom Guinzburg, Arthur Miller, Saul Bellow, John
Steinbeck at a reception in the publisher's offices to celebrate
Steinbeck's Nobel Prize in Literature in 1964. At that gathering,
Steinbeck inscribed a copy of *Herzog*, published that year:
"Dear Saul: You're next."

Medallion: Nobel Prize in Literature 1976.

At the Nobel Ball with son Daniel, December 10, 1976.

Sunday, December 12, 1976, at Swedish publisher Gerard Bonnier's luncheon in honor of Saul Bellow and before his formal Nobel Lecture later that afternoon at the Stock Exchange in Stockholm. In front row, (l. to r.): publisher Tom Guinzburg; Saul; UK publisher Barley Alison; Gerard Bonnier; German publisher Reinhold Neven Du Mont.

At the National Arts Club award of Gold Medal in Literature to Saul Bellow, (l. to r.) Dick Cavett, Saul, Bernard Malamud talking with photographer Tom Victor (obscured), and longtime friend John Cheever.

Bernard Malamud reading appreciation at ceremony.

On the set of PBS' Great Performances film of *Seize the Day*, with Robin Williams, who upon meeting SB asked: "Do you have the Nobel Prize on you?"

Early Sunday morning, June 10, 1984, Lachine, Quebec, with niece Lesha, in front of 130 Eighth Avenue, the house in which Saul was born, sixty-nine years earlier to the day, stopping by before the big event at the Bibliotheque Municipal Saul Bellow. The staircase leads to the second-floor apartment next door of Aunt Rosa, Uncle Max, and the cousins Gameroff.

NOVEMBER 18, 1984

Family Weekly

OUR SECOND
ANNUAL
NATIONAL
TREASURE
AWARDS

HELEN HAYES     SAUL BELLOW     CORETTA SCOTT KING     ARTHUR MILLER     DR. NORMAN VINCENT PEALE

Co-winner of Family Weekly 1984 National Treasure Award (nominations made by 365 Sunday newspapers across the country). "Bellow's novels are a repository of the American spirit, expressed neither in the King's nor in Webster's English, but in the urbanized vernacular of the streets of Chicago."

Svenska Akademien
har vid sitt sammanträde
den 21 oktober 1976
i överensstämmelse med
föreskrifterna i det av
ALFRED NOBEL
den 27 november 1895
upprättade testamente
beslutat att tilldela
Saul Bellow
1976 års nobelpris i litteratur
för den mänskliga förståelse
och subtila kulturanalys
som förenas i hans verk.

STOCKHOLM DEN 10 DECEMBER 1976

Actual award and original painting presented by the King at ceremony.

December 13, Santa Lucia Day in Sweden. Saul Bellow is award-ed a kiss by 1976 Queen of Lights at outdoor coronation, snow flakes falling.

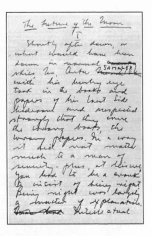

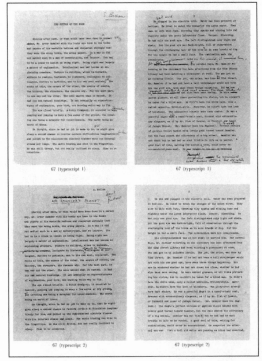

Sotheby catalog, June 8, 1988, auction of creative archive for *Mr. Sammler's Planet*, originally titled *The Future of the Moon*, (notebook covers, typescript pages before and after editing, holograph of first page).

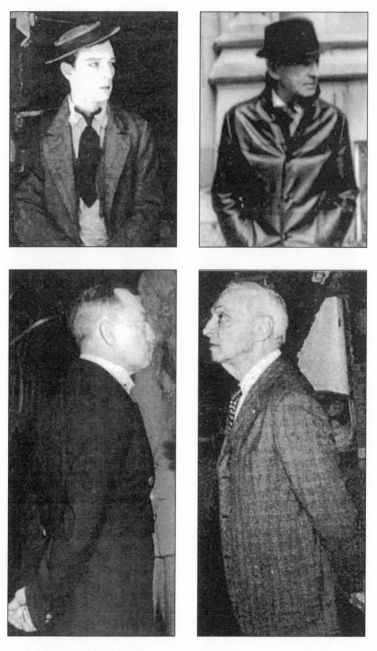

Separated at birth? Buster Keaton and Saul Bellow, nicknamed
"Buster" in high school.

This "being human" is our very own show. All that mankind is said to be, pro or contra, comes from mankind itself. Everything that we can possibly conceive is made into fact, and it all comes out of bottomless reservoirs of our invention and fantasy.

Mozart Bicentennial Address
Florence, Italy December 1, 1992